W9-CRO-888

MY BOOK HOUSE
THE LATCH KEY

THE LATCH KEY

HERE stands a house all built of thought,
And full to overflowing
Of treasures and of precious things,
Of secrets for my knowing.

Its windows look out far and wide
From each of all its stories.
I'll take the key and enter in;
For me are all its glories.

THE LATCH KEY
of MY BOOKHOUSE

Edited by
Olive Beaupré Miller

CHICAGO
The BOOKHOUSE for CHILDREN
PUBLISHERS

H

Printed in U. S. A.

CONTENTS OF THE LATCH KEY

What the child admired,
The youth endeavored and the
man acquired.
—John Dryden
G. K.

AESOP (Greek, About 619–564 B. C.)

SOMEWHERE in ancient Greece, the land of white-pillared cities and stately marble temples, was born the little slave boy, Aesop. While he was still a child, Aesop was brought to the far-famed city of Athens. There he was sold, like an ox or a sheep, from one master to another and performed in each household the hard and thankless duties of a slave. Nevertheless, he was always enlivening his tasks by the brightest and cleverest sallies of wit, which often threw his comrades into gales of laughter.

Once, it is said, he and his fellow slaves were about to set out on a long journey with a certain merchant who was their master. Heavy bundles of necessary clothing and provisions were prepared for each of the slaves to carry.

"Master, grant me to carry the lightest bundle," cried Aesop.

"Sobeit! Select the lightest," his master answered.

Immediately Aesop stepped forward and chose the heaviest and most unwieldy package of all, a bulky basket of bread. His comrades laughed at what they considered his foolishness, but when the noon meal came Aesop was ordered to distribute half his loaves among the party. Thus his load was lightened at the very time when the burdens of the others began to seem heavier and heavier from their having borne them so long. By supper time Aesop was ordered to distribute the rest of his bread and for the remainder of the journey he had nothing left to carry but the empty basket. His companions, as they trudged on, perspiring and weary, could not but admit that they had been the foolish ones and in spite of their burdens, they smiled at the joke which Aesop's quick wit and foresight had played upon their stupidity.

At last the young slave's cleverness caught the attention of his master, Iadmon, the Samian, and as a fitting reward, Iadmon set him free. Thereupon, Aesop journeyed to the magnificent court of Croesus, King of Lydia, with whom he came into high favor.

Thenceforward, during the rest of his life, he who had been born a slave associated intimately with the greatest men of letters of his day, and none among them could turn a fable so perfectly as he, could pack so much truth into a story so short, pithy and exactly to the point.

At length Aesop was sent as the ambassador of Croesus to Delphi, with instructions to pay a certain sum of money to each of the citizens there. On his arrival, however, he found the Delphians to be in some fault and fell into a dispute with them. As the discussion waxed warmer and warmer, he flatly refused to distribute the money. Incensed at his conduct, the Delphians accused him of sacrilege and hurled him headlong from a precipice to his death.

People have always insisted on believing that, in appearance, Aesop was a monster of ugliness and deformity, and so he is most often represented. This story, however, appears to be utterly without foundation and was probably invented long after his death, merely to make his wit seem more remarkable by contrast with such deformity. In truth, Aesop must have been unusually handsome, since we are told that the Athenians erected in his honor a noble statue, by the famous sculptor, Lysippus.

None of Aesop's works remain today. How many of the fables attributed to him were actually his is extremely uncertain. His tales were probably never written down but were passed about from mouth to mouth, just as men tell a good story today. Walking two and two in the market place, or beneath the splendid porticoes of the public baths, the ancient Athenians repeated these fables to each other and chuckled over their cleverness, exactly as men enjoy telling each other witty stories to this very day. They were popular in Athens during the most brilliant period of its literary history. Originally they were in prose, but in time were put into verse by various Greek and Latin poets. The most famous of these Latin poets was Phaedrus who lived at Rome in

the first century A. D. Mere scraps of these early versions, however, remain. In the fourteenth century, the monk Maximus Planudes made a collection which he gave out as Aesop's, but the truth is that he added to Aesop's fables a number taken from oriental sources. It is from this collection that the modern fables, as we know them, have been derived. Through all the ages no name shines more brightly for sage and clever wit than that of Aesop. *Aesop for Children, illustrated by Milo Winter*

ALCOTT,* LOUISA MAY (American, 1832–1888)

In the historic old town of Concord, Massachusetts, there lived once a strong, sturdy, jolly girl named Louisa Alcott. Louisa's home was a shabby, dingy old house, but it was full of simple happiness and its four bare walls rang often with shouts of merry laughter. For Louisa had the tenderest, most loving mother imaginable, a wise, devoted father and three lively sisters, Anna, Beth and May. Over the hills behind old Concord, whence the green meadows swept away to meet the golden sunset, and down by the rush-bordered river that went slowly meandering through the town, the little girls loved to romp and play.

*Read the Life of Louisa May Alcott by Belle Moses

THE LATCH KEY

They weren't very well off, so far as money goes, those Alcotts. Mr. Alcott was a school teacher with an immense love for children and a beautiful way of teaching them, but he believed very earnestly that people should lead simpler, truer, more useful lives than they do, and his opinions as to how they should set about doing this were so different from those held by others that men laughed at him and said he was odd and would not send their children to his school. Moreover, he said plainly that the owning of slaves was wrong, and this made him still more unpopular in an age when, even in the North, men were not ready at all to agree with him. So he found it very difficult indeed to get along. But Mr. Alcott was the sort of man who was always loyal to the best ideas he knew and would cling to them with his whole strength, no matter what it cost him. Shoulder to shoulder with him stood his brave wife, always upholding him, working day and night with her capable hands to make his burdens lighter, cooking, sewing, cleaning. And in spite of all the hard work she did, she was never too tired to be gay and jolly and interested in all that interested her daughters. So the four little girls were brought up from their infancy in a world of simple living and high thinking. They had plenty of joyous, carefree fun in which both mother and father joined, but they began to understand very early the necessity for being useful and bearing their share in the household tasks. Thus, though the house where they lived was poor and shabby, it was very rich in love and loyalty and simple homey joys.

Louisa was a strong, active, handsome girl with blue eyes and a perfect mane of heavy chestnut hair. She could run for miles and miles and never get tired and she was as sturdy as a boy. Indeed, her mother used sometimes to call her Jo in fun and say that Jo was

her only son. Jo loved to climb trees and leap fences, run races and roll hoops, and when she was not playing with her sisters she liked best to play with boys. But beside all these lively sports, Louisa liked, too, to curl herself up in a chair and read or study. Sometimes she would go off alone up into the garret, taking a pile of apples with her and her favorite book. There she would read and munch away in happy solitude. All day long she had interesting thoughts and often she wrote these down in her diary. She used to make up stories, too, and tell them to her sisters.

On occasion, little Louisa could be a turbulent miss and her high spirits often led her into paths of strange adventure. Once, when she was very small and lived in Boston, she ran away from home and spent the day with some Irish children. They shared a very poor and very salty dinner with her, after which they all went to play in the nice, dirty, ash heaps. Late in the afternoon they took a daring trip as far away as Boston Common. When it began to grow dark, however, Louisa's little Irish friends deserted her, and there she was left all alone in a strange place with the dusky shadows deepening and the night lights twinkling out. Then, indeed, she began to long for home, but she hadn't the smallest idea which way to go and so wandered helplessly on and on. At last, quite wearied out, she sat down on a welcome doorstep beside a friendly big dog. The dog kindly allowed her to use his back for a pillow and she fell fast asleep. From her dreams she was roused by the voice of the town crier who had been sent in search of her by her distracted parents. He was ringing his bell and calling out loudly, "Lost! Lost! A little girl six years old in a pink frock, white hat and new green shoes!"

Out of the darkness a small voice answered him, "Why dat's me!"

Next day the little runaway was tied to the arm of a sofa to cure her of her wandering habit.

When naughty traits of character got the better of Louisa, however, she always suffered intensely in her own little heart for the wrong she had done. In the intervals of working off steam in the liveliest adventures, she was often sadly troubled by her faults. Sometimes, then, she had a little game she would play. She liked to make believe that she was a princess and that her kingdom was her own mind. When she had hateful, self-willed or dissatisfied thoughts, she tried to get rid of these by playing that they were enemies of her kingdom. She would marshal her legions of soldiers and march them bravely against the foe. Her soldiers, she said, were Patience, Duty and Love. With these she fought her battles and drove out the enemy. When she was only fourteen years old she wrote a poem about this.

A little kingdom I possess,
Where thoughts and feelings dwell,
And very hard I find the task
Of governing it well.

Nevertheless, after many a hotly contested battle, she did succeed in taking command and governing her kingdom like a queen.

The house where the four girls lived in Concord had a yard full of fine old trees and a big barn which was their most particular delight. Here they produced many marvelous plays, for Anna and Louisa both had a wonderful talent for acting. They made the barn into a theatre and climbed up on the haymow for a stage. The grown people who came to see their plays would sit on chairs on the floor. One of the children's favorite plays was Jack and the Beanstalk. They had a ladder from the floor to the loft, and all the way up the ladder they tied a squash vine to look like the wonderful beanstalk. When it came to the place in the story where Jack was fleeing from the giant and the giant was hot on his heels, about to plunge down the beanstalk, the girl who took the part of Jack would cut down the vine with a mighty flourish while the audience held their breath. Then, crashing out of the loft to his well-deserved end below, would come the monstrous old giant. This giant was made of pillows dressed in a suit of funny old clothes, with a fierce, hideous head made of paper.

Another play which the children acted was Cinderella. They made a big pumpkin out of the wheelbarrow trimmed with yellow paper. Thus the pumpkin could easily become a golden coach in which Cinderella magnificently rolled away at a single stroke of the fairy godmother's wand. The tale of the foolish woman who wasted her three wishes was illustrated in a way to make the beholders scream with laughter, by means of a pudding which was lowered by invisible hands until it rested upon the poor lady's nose.

The costumes used in these performances were marvelous affairs, for Louisa, Anna and Mrs. Alcott had a wonderful knack for rigging up something out of nothing. A scrap found its use. A bright colored scarf, a table cover, a bit of old lace, a long cloak, a big hat with a plume stolen from some departed bonnet, would afford a regal costume in which to come sweeping on to the stage. The children were never at a lack, either, for scenery, for their ready wit was quite capable of providing castles, enchanted forests, caves or ladies' bowers. Barns offered splendid opportunities, too, for a hero or a villain to make desperate but safe leaps from the beams, or to sink out of sight, at short notice, into one of the various mangers, and hence they had everything necessary right at hand.

There was one other beautiful and much more serious story which the Alcott children loved to play, though they did not give this to an audience in the barn, but played it alone for their own amusement. This story was Pilgrim's Progress, in which the pilgrim, Christian, loaded down with his burden of sins, finds his way through toil and danger from the City of Destruction to the Celestial City. Their mother used to tie her piece-bags on their backs to represent Christian's burden. Then they would put on broad-brimmed, pilgrim hats, take a stick for a staff and start out on their journey. From the cellar, which was the City of Destruction, they would mount to the housetop where was the Celestial City, and they would act out on the way, in most dramatic form, every step of Christian's upward progress. Sometimes, instead of playing Pilgrim's Progress indoors they would play it out of doors, wandering over the hills behind the house, through the woods and down the lanes. Louisa loved all these plays and, besides the old ones which they performed, she made up some new ones of her own, very thrilling and tragic and therefore, very funny.

There could not have been a more beautiful place than Concord

for four hearty, simple girls like these to live. It was a typical New England village, quiet and homelike, with its plain, white houses and its shady elm trees, nestling in its circle of peaceful hills. There were no very rich people there and none very poor. The inhabitants were honest and friendly, with simple occupations and amusements and very few worldly ambitions. In the winter the place used to ring with the happy voices of young people skating on the hardened snow in the pine woods. In the summer the river would be alive with gay bathing or boating parties. Concord was an historic old place, too, with its memories of the first gun-shots of the Revolution, and many a time in the days of the Alcott girls, there used to be masquerades on the fine old river to celebrate the anniversary of that great event. Gay barges full of historic characters in costume would glide down the stream, and sometimes savages in their war-paint would dart from the lily-fringed river banks to attack the gay masqueraders. Hearty and healthy was the life in Concord and it produced a fine race of people, among them three, at least, of most remarkable character. These three were Emerson, Hawthorne and Thoreau, and though these men were much older than Louisa, they were all of them her friends.

Ralph Waldo Emerson was one of the greatest men in the history of American literature. He was a thinker, a philosopher and a poet, strong, gentle and serene. He had stood by Mr. Alcott when everybody else laughed at him and deserted him, and from her earliest recollections Louisa had adored him. Once she went to school with the little Emersons in their father's barn, for in those days of no public schools, teachers used frequently to gather their pupils together in barns. The illustrious Mr. Emerson was often the children's playfellow. He would pile all the youngsters on a great hay-cart and take them off to picnic or go berrying in the woods. Emerson's friend, Henry Thoreau, who loved the tangled depths of the forests, had once gone off and lived by himself in a hut that he built on the edge of Walden Pond, to prove to himself and others the joy of utterly simple living, close to the heart of Nature. The hut was in a beautiful spot among fragrant pines and overlooked the clear, green depths of the pond which Thoreau, from its gleaming expressiveness, called the eye of the earth. About Walden Pond, encircling it everywhere, rose the hills, the tall, green hills. To this beautiful spot Emerson used to take the children. He would show them all the places he loved, all the wood people Thoreau had introduced to him, or the wildflowers whose hidden homes he had discovered. So, years later, when the children read Emerson's beautiful poem about the sweet rhodora in the woods, his "burly, dozing bumblebee," or laughed over the fable of the Mountain and the Squirrel, they recognized old friends of these beautiful woodland jaunts and thanked Emerson for the delicate truth and beauty he had seen there and helped them to understand.

To the turbulent, restless, half-grown Louisa the calm philosopher, with his gentle ways and practical common-sense, was an anchor indeed. In her warm little heart he was held so sacredly that he himself would have smiled at such worship. She went to him often for advice about her reading and was at liberty to roam all around the book-lined walls of his library, there to select whatever pleased her most, for Emerson was never too busy to help her.

Hawthorne, too, handsome shy man that he was, always steering away from the society of grown-ups, had much to do with Louisa and the Concord children. He was always at his best with children and his stories never failed to hold Louisa spellbound. Doubtless she was one of the children to whom he first told the *Tanglewood Tales* and the stories in the *Wonder Book*. She pored over his books, and love and admiration for him grew with her growth.

Henry Thoreau was the last of those great Concord friends who had such an influence on Louisa's life. From him the Alcott girls learned to know intimately the nature they already loved, and many a happy day was spent with him in the woods, studying the secrets of the wildflowers and the language of the birds. It was down by the river that Thoreau was most often to be found. There he would row his boat or paddle his canoe with Indian skill through the many windings, stopping now and then to gather some rare plant from among the grasses on the shore. In his company the girls would take long, long walks, too, even tramping the twenty miles from Concord to Boston. There was not a single flower or tree that the gentle woodsman did not know; birds, squirrels and insects were his comrades. Hunted foxes would come to him for protection; wild squirrels would nestle in his coat; birds and chipmunks gathered about him as he sat at rest on the river bank; he seemed able even to coax the fishes up to the surface to feed out of his hand. And so for him all Nature had a voice, and the Concord children loved the simple friend who taught them the poetry of the woods.

As Louisa grew up into a tall young girl she began to come into prominence as a story teller. Her nature studies gave her material, and out in the Concord woods she would gather about her the little Emerson children, Ellen, Edith and Edward, and the three Hawthorne children, Una, Julian and Rose, and many another, too. Then, under the spreading branches of some great tree, with the sunshine filtering down on her head and lighting up all the eager little faces about her, she would tell stories that made the very woods alive—wood-sprites and water-sprites and fairy queens dancing in and out through the greenery of those cool forest glades.

But in spite of all the delights of Concord, Louisa was beginning to feel the weight of the family troubles. She saw her father struggling day by day, earning a little here and there by the work of his hands when his talents as a teacher were running to waste. She saw her mother carrying burdens too heavy for her and working far too hard. She had always helped her mother all she could with the housework, but the greatest need of the household now was for more money. A noble purpose took root in Louisa's heart. She would set out into the world, earn a living, and mend the family fortunes. She would give this dear devoted mother the comforts

that had been denied her so long. Once determined to accomplish this, Louisa never rested. True, she was only a girl, and there were very few lines of activity open to girls in those days. The way seemed dark before her and full of obstacles. But Louisa was never daunted. Full of energy and pluck, she set forth. First she went up to Boston and lived in a wretched little sky-parlor. There she wrote stories for various magazines and papers, taught in a kindergarten and did sewing or anything else that came to her hand. Only one thing mattered to her henceforth, to help her mother, father and sisters. Night and day she worked, never sparing herself, and every penny that she did not absolutely need for the barest necessities of life, she sent home to her mother and father. James Russell Lowell was the editor of the *Atlantic Monthly* in those days and he praised her stories and took them for his magazine. Yet, as the years passed, she wrote nothing that had any very lasting merit. She merely labored unceasingly and earned money enough by her own self-sacrifice to keep her dear ones in greater comfort at home.

Then one day Louisa's publisher asked her to write a book for girls. Louisa was very worn and weary, and she hadn't the smallest idea that she could really write an interesting book for children. All these years she had written for grown-ups only. But she had never yet said "I can't" when she was asked to do anything. So, in spite of her misgivings she answered the publishers simply, "I'll try." When she began to think about what she should write, she remembered all the good times she used to have with her sisters in the big, bare house in Concord, out in the old barn, and over the hills. So she wrote the story of *Little Women* and put in all those things. Besides the jolly times and the plays they had, she put in the sad, hard times too, the work and the worry and the going without things. It was a simple story of simple girls, of their daily struggles, their joys and sorrows, but through it all shone the spirit of that beautiful family affection that the Alcotts knew so well, an affection so strong and enduring that neither poverty, sorrow, nor death could ever mar it. And the little book was so sweet and funny, so sad and real, like human life, that everybody bought it and much money came from it.

There were Mr. and Mrs. March in the book, true as life to Mr. and Mrs. Alcott, and there were all the four sisters too. Meg, the capable house-wifely one, was Anna; Jo (the old pet name for Louisa) was Louisa, herself, the turbulent, boyish one, who was always "going into a vortex" and writing stories; Beth was the sweet, sunny little home-body, Lizzie or Beth; Amy was May, the pretty, golden-haired, blue-eyed one, with the artistic tastes, whose pug nose was such a sore trial to her beauty-loving soul that she went about with a clothespin on it to train it into proper lines. There was a real John Brooke, too. He was a portrait of that gentle, kindly, lovable John Pratt, who really married Anna. And Laurie was a mixture of a handsome, polished, Polish boy whom Louisa had once met in Europe, and a certain New England lad who was her friend in girlhood. So, many of the good times in *Little Women* are true, and many of the sad times too,—the marriage of Meg and John Brooke, and the death of dear little Beth.

Louisa was hardly prepared for the immense success of this book. It made her almost rich, and besides that, she suddenly found herself so worshiped and idolized by young people and old alike, that crowds began haunting her path, hanging about the house to get just a glimpse of her—popping up in her way to bow reverently as she went for a walk or a drive, deluging her with flowers, and writing her sentimental verses. All this attention drove Louisa nearly distracted, so she had to run away from it for a year's rest in Europe. But ever after that the children considered Louisa their especial property and she devoted herself henceforth to writing for them entirely. She loved them very dearly, too, boys and girls alike, and no American author has ever held a warmer place than she in the hearts of American young people.

And so, after so many years of the hardest, most devoted and unselfish labor, Louisa's dream came true. She was able to give her dear family all that they needed and wanted. She bought a comfortable home for them in Concord, she sent May to study art in Europe, she gave her father books, but best of all, she was able at last to give her beloved mother the happiness and rest which she had so nobly earned. Never again did "Marmee" have to do any hard work. She could sit from that time forth in a comfortable chair beside the sunny window with beautiful work and beauiful things about her. A successful life was Louisa Alcott's, one of toil and effort, indeed, of joy and sorrow, and ceaseless self-sacrifice, but through it all, as through *Little Women* ran the golden thread of that splendid family love.

Important Works: *Little Women* *Little Men* *Jo's Boys* *An Old-fashioned Girl* *Jack and Jill* *Eight Cousins* *Rose In Bloom* *Silver Pitchers*

ALDEN, RAYMOND MacDONALD (American, 1873–)

Raymond MacDonald Alden was born at Hartford, New York, and educated at Rollins College, Florida, the University of Pennsylvania, and Harvard. He has edited several plays by Shakespeare and the Elizabethan dramatists, and has taught as instructor and professor at Harvard, Leland Stanford, Jr. and the Universities of Pennsylvania and Illinois. He was director of the Drama League of America from its founding until 1914.

Important Works: *Why The Chimes Rang*

ALDRICH, THOMAS BAILEY
(American, 1836–1907)

THOMAS BAILEY ALDRICH was born in the quaint, old, elm-shaded town of Portsmouth, New Hampshire, which lies so near to the ocean that the constant sight of tall-masted ships and the smell of the sea are enough to set any boy's blood a-tingle with the spirit of adventure.

As a boy Tom was very fond of reading. He spent whole hours in the attic of the old house where he lived, and there from the midst of castaway rubbish, he dug out such books of adventure as Don Quixote, Arabian Nights, and various works of Defoe.

Among the antiquated furniture in the attic, too, was an old-fashioned, hide-covered trunk, reminiscent of those fascinating days long past. The trunk had worn exceedingly shabby, but still had enough of the air of romance about it to be very interesting to Tom. One day, as the boy was passing a barber's shop, he saw some hair restorer displayed in the window, in connection with marvelous promises as to what the same could do in the matter of restoring hair where none seemed to be. Thinking of his beloved but moth-eaten trunk, Tom went into the shop immediately and parted with what must have seemed an enormous amount of his pocket money, to buy a bottle of the hair restorer. He then returned at once to his attic and began applying the liquid copiously to the hide of the trunk, in eager hopes of seeing new hair appear in the bald places. Every day, thereafter, he patiently climbed the stairs to observe the expected sprouting. But strange to say, the old trunk remained as bald as before!

THE LATCH KEY

Before he was twelve years old, Tom had written a pirate story called by the highly exciting name of Colenzo. The scene of this thrilling tale was a wild, lonely and tropical isle located, according to Tom, somewhere about seven miles off Portsmouth Harbor!

When Tom was sixteen, his father died, and there was no money to send the boy to college, so he set out to seek his fortune in New York. There he became a clerk in the office of an uncle who was a banker. All the time, however, the impulse which had prompted him to write Colenzo was urging and urging within him, so that, by the time he was twenty, he had decided to break away from the business world altogether and devote himself to writing as a profession. At first it was by no means easy sailing, trying to earn a living by writing. He obtained work as a proof-reader in a publishing house, to make both ends meet, but he stuck pluckily to his profession and at last found himself editor of one of the well known magazines. From that time on he was always a prominent figure in the literary world.

For many years he was a writer both of prose and of such lovely poems as *Robins in the Treetop*. He was also the editor, at different times, of various magazines, including the New York *Illustrated News* and the *Atlantic Monthly*. But always Tom's boyhood and the happy days of boyish adventure and fancy in Portsmouth were with him. Rivermouth, the scene of several of his stories, is really Portsmouth, and in *The Story of a Bad Boy*, he tells much that was true of his own boyhood.

In the old Aldrich home at Portsmouth visitors may see, to this very day, the marvelous ship and the little room that were Tom's, and in the garret, the playthings of which he tells and which he so dearly loved.

Important Works: The Story of a Bad Boy
Marjorie Daw

ALLINGHAM, WILLIAM (Irish, 1824–1889)

Allingham was an Irish poet, born at Ballyshannon in the county of Donegal, a country whose very name suggests Irish imagination and all the eerie atmosphere of Ireland's fairy lore. He was an intimate friend of Tennyson, Dante Gabriel Rossetti, Leigh Hunt and all the rest of that splendid company of English poets who made the reign of Queen Victoria one of the greatest periods in English literature. But for all his longer and more pretentious works, Allingham is remembered today chiefly for just those few graceful little poems that nearly every child knows, *The Fairies, The Song of the Leprechaun,* and *Robin Redbreast*

Important Works: Day and Night Songs Rhymes for Young Folks

ALMA-TADEMA, SIR LAWRENCE (Belgian–English, 1836–1912)

In the year 1836 there was born of a very old and wealthy Dutch family in the Netherlands, a small boy named Lawrence Alma-Tadema. When he was old enough to go to school Lawrence was sent to Antwerp to study, and there he very soon began to show a wonderful talent for drawing. He grew eagerly interested, too, in old Greek and Roman tables and chairs and lamps and everything else that had to do with the days of long ago. How the old Greeks lived when the Acropolis crowned a busy city humming with life, what the Romans did when the Forum was a center of bustling activity—all this fascinated him and he kept on studying it and investigating it until, by and by, he began to paint the most interesting pictures on those subjects.

When he was still a very young man he went to England and in 1873 he became a British subject. During all the rest of his life he lived in London and hence he is classed among British artists. Though Alma-Tadema wrote some beautiful poems which all children know, he is remembered chiefly for his paintings. These pictures are vivid scenes from the everyday life of the ancients, such as, "How They Amused Themselves in Egypt Three Thousand Years Ago," "A Roman Dance," etc.

THE LATCH KEY

ANDERSEN, HANS CHRISTIAN (Danish, 1805–1875)

It matters not to have been born in a duck-yard if one has been hatched from a swan's egg.

A HUNDRED years or more ago there lived in the ancient city of Odense in Denmark, an awkward, overgrown, lean little boy. Hans Andersen's father was a cobbler, his mother a washerwoman, and they were so poor that they lived in one room under a steep gabled roof. That room had to be kitchen and parlor, workshop and bedroom all in one, but, poor as it was, it was to Hans most wonderfully exciting. In every corner it was full of interesting things. The walls were covered with pictures; the tables and chests had shiny cups, glasses and jugs upon them; in the lattice window grew pots of mint; from the rafters hung bunches of sweet herbs, and there were always fresh green boughs hanging here and there about. Over by the window, where the sun streamed in, was the cobbler's work-bench and a shelf of books. But most interesting of all to Hans was the door of the room which was brightly painted with pictures—fields and hedges, trees and houses, perhaps even castles — and when the little boy had gone to bed and his mother and father thought him fast asleep, he would lie awake to look at those pictures and make up stories about them. Often, too, in the day time he would crawl up the ladder and out on the roof of the house where in the gutter between the Andersen's cottage and the one next door, there stood a box of earth in which Hans's mother had planted chives and parsley. This was their garden, for all the world like Kay and Gerda's garden in the *Snow Queen*.

Hans's father, though he passed his days pounding pegs into shoes, was a very well educated man, who had seen far better days. He loved to read and spent all his spare time with his books. This made him seem very different from his poor neighbors, and even

from his wife who had no education at all. He and Hans were great friends and they often went on long walks together. While the father sat and thought or read, Hans ran about and gathered wild strawberries or made pretty garlands of flowers. It was from his father that the boy got his love for reading and his rich and vivid fancy. Nevertheless, though Hans liked to read. he did no other lessons at all, for he did not like other studies.

As a child he would play all alone out in the tiny garden behind the house. For hours he would sit near their one gooseberry bush where, with the help of a broomstick and his mother's apron, he had made a little tent. Under this shelter he would sit cozily in all kinds of weather, fancying things and inventing stories. His father had made him some wonderful toys, pictures that changed their shape when pulled with a string, a mill which made the miller dance when it turned around, and a peepshow of funny rag dolls. Hans liked best of all to play with this little toy theatre, for he was unusually fond of plays. He would dress up these little rag puppets and very seriously make them go through the actions of many a thrilling drama.

Occasionally, though very seldom, the boy went to school. Once he made friends at school with a little girl, to whom he told many remarkable stories. These stories were chiefly about himself, and his favorite one was how he was of noble birth only the fairies had changed him in his cradle and nobody knew the truth about him! One day he heard the little girl say, "Hans is a fool." Poor little Hans! He trembled and told her no more stories.

When Hans was only eleven years old his father died and he was left alone with his mother. He still continued to play with his toy theatre, but he also now read everything on which he could lay his hands. Best of all he loved to read Shakespeare, and Shakespeare left a deep impression upon him. He liked particularly those plays of Shakespeare's where there were ghosts or witches, and indeed he became so devotedly fond of the drama that he felt he must be an actor. Sometimes he decided that he could sing unusually well and should make his fortune by acting and singing. One day an old woman who was washing clothes in the river told Hans that the Empire of China lay down there under the water. Having taken no pains to learn anything about the world, Hans quite believed her and thought to himself that perhaps, some moonlight night when he should be singing down by the water's edge, a Chinese prince, charmed by his marvelous music, would push his way up through the earth and take him down to China to make him rich and noble as a reward for such unsurpassed singing. Then the prince might let him return some day to Odense, where he would be very rich and build himself a castle, to be envied and admired by all who had once despised him!

Naturally enough, young Hans singing in the lanes, reading and playing theatre alone by himself at home, was despised and

regarded almost as a lunatic by the people of Odense. Tall, gawky boy that he was, with a huge nose, tiny eyes and a great long neck like a bird's, with feet and hands as big as boats, and clothes always too small for him—he was the laughing stock of the neighborhood. Boys teased him and screamed after him, "There goes the play scribbler." Wounded to the quick, Hans shrank away from them all and hid himself at home, safe from their mockery. He had not a single friend of his own age in Odense.

The gentry who lived round about, though they were amused by the cobbler's peculiar son, were also sorry for him. They laughed at his absurd ambitions to be a great writer, a singer or actor, when he had never taken the trouble to get the smallest education, but they tried, too, to induce him to go to school. For a time he did as they wished, but in school he was always dreamy and absent-minded, studying little, and he tried to please his master by bringing him wild flowers instead of learning his lessons.

At length, at the age of fourteen, he came to the conclusion like the heroes he had read about in his books, that he would set out and seek his fortune. This meant that he would go to Copenhagen and there find work at the theatre. He had heard of a wonderful thing called a ballet which seemed to him grander and finer than anything else in the world, and of a marvelous lady who danced in the ballet. Hans pictured this chief dancer as a sort of fairy queen, who should graciously condescend to help him and, by a wave of her hand, make him famous.

His mother was rather alarmed at these plans of the lad, so she sought advice from a fortune-teller. But that wise woman, after consulting the coffee grounds, solemnly announced that Hans Christian Andersen would be a great man and that all Odense would one day be illumined to do him honor! This statement seemed ridiculous and was received with many a wink and shrug of the shoulders by others, but it satisfied Hans's mother and she consented to let him go. So the boy confidently did up his little bundle, and with nine dollars in his pocket, took ship for Copenhagen.

Once arrived in the city, he hurried off to find his fairy queen, the chief dancer, and poured out in her wondering ears his longing to go on the stage. To show her what he could do, he took off his shoes and began dancing about in his stocking feet, using his hat for a drum and beating a lively tattoo! Needless to say, the graceful gambols of this overgrown giraffe terrified the poor lady. She took him for a lunatic and hastily showed him the door.

In spite of this disappointment, however, Hans persisted. He went to seek help from the Director of the Theatre, only to meet here with another rebuff. He was told that none but educated people were engaged for the stage. So began the long series of Hans's adventures and disappointments. Ridiculous as he appeared to others, he sincerely respected himself and had a firm belief in his own ability to do something. But he was keenly sensitive, too, and the constant rebuffs he met with always hurt him sorely. All the unhappiness of those days, as well as of his childhood, he expressed years later in the story of the Ugly Duckling, whose buffetings and miseries represent his own early trials.

He lived now in a garret in the poorest quarter of Copenhagen and had nothing to eat but a cup of coffee in the morning and a roll later in the day. Though he found friends who even then recognized his talent and wished to help him, he would not take from them more than was absolutely necessary. He would pretend that he had had plenty to eat and that he had been dining out with friends, rather than accept more of their charity. He would say, too, that he was quite warm when his clothes were threadbare and his boots so worn and leaky that his feet were sopping with water. The courage and determination he showed at this time were really remarkable in a lad of fifteen. He once sent a play he had written to the Royal Theatre, never doubting in his childish ignorance that it would be accepted. It came back to him very soon with the curt comment that it showed such a lack of education as to be absolutely absurd. Nothing daunted, however, he wrote another play and tried again. This time those who read his manuscript at the theatre said that it showed unmistakable signs of talent, and they advised Andersen's friends to ask the King for money to educate the boy.

Frederick VI of Denmark was like the kind kings in Andersen's stories. He arranged at once that Hans should be sent to school, and from then on he helped the boy until he was able to take care of himself. Hans was not happy in school, however. Here he was, a great hulking lad of seventeen, having to go into classes with the very smallest boys. He had plenty of opportunity then to wish that he had applied himself earlier to his lessons. But though he worked hard, both here and later at the University in Copenhagen, he found it difficult to learn, and was generally thought a dunce. He continued to write poems, plays and sketches, which were all pronounced wishy-washy and silly. He failed again and again. Yet in the very bottom of his heart, in spite of all his failures, something always said, "I can," and his faith in himself never faltered.

At length, Frederick VI allowed him money for foreign travel, and he set forth to visit Italy, France and Germany. In Italy he found his inspiration for his first really successful novel, *The Improvisatore*, which was published on his return to Copenhagen.

During all this time Andersen had been looking solely to his novels and plays to win him success and recognition. But while he was doing work of the most ordinary merit in this line he had one admirable talent which he never even dreamed of taking seriously. Odense, his birthplace, was a rich treasure house of legends and folk lore, and sometimes, just to amuse the children of his friends, he would gather the little ones about him and weave these old legends into the most wonderful stories. He would tell these tales in the liveliest manner, never bothering about grammar but using childish words and baby language, and as he talked he would act and jump about and make the most remarkable faces. The children were

simply delighted. At length, Andersen's friends suggested that he write down these stories. At first he laughed at such an idea, but finally he consented, more in fun than in earnest. So he wrote the stories exactly as he told them. This made them different from anything else that had ever been published in Denmark. Most people when they write have a formal, stilted manner, quite different from their ordinary conversation, but Andersen's tales were written in the same lively, simple, informal style in which he had told them. In this lay their particular charm. The critics, of course,—those who were not too grand even to look at such childish trash—criticized the stories for this informal style and bewailed the lack of elegance in their wording.

Even Andersen himself did not take these "small things" seriously, and yet it was his fairy tales and nothing else that won him his lasting fame. In them he gave free rein to his wonderful fancy and embodied all the childlike simplicity of his great and loving heart. Soon the stories became so popular that they were translated into one foreign language after another, and while Andersen's novels and plays have long since been forgotten, it is due to his fairy tales that he is still more widely read than any other Scandinavian writer. Children pore over these stories to this very day, from America to India, from Greenland to South Africa.

The recognition thus won by Andersen after so many years of struggle was, to him, a source of constant wonder and delight. That he, the son of a poor washerwoman and a cobbler, should now be the friend of princes and kings, seemed to him more marvelous than the most fantastic incidents of his own fairy tales. Often, when he was enjoying some quite ordinary luxury which most people take for granted, such as lying on a sofa in a new dressing gown, surrounded by books, he would think of his childhood and wonder. On his travels, too, he found himself welcomed everywhere and met on the friendliest terms by the greatest literary men of his day. In France he met Dumas and Victor Hugo, in Germany, the brothers Grimm, in England, Charles Dickens, and his simple, childlike nature drew all people to love him. Now, when he passed along the streets of Copenhagen, those who saw him would nudge each other and say, "There goes the great poet!" Quite different from the days when the boys had shrieked after him, "There goes the play scribbler!"

On December sixth, 1867, when Andersen was sixty two years old, the prophecy made so long ago to his mother was fulfilled. In Odense, the city of his birth, the once scorned and ugly little boy was greeted with an immense celebration. To do him honor all the town, from end to end, was one great blaze of light. And so, at last, the ugly duckling turned out, in very truth, to be a swan.

Important Works: Andersen's Fairy Tales The Improvisatore

ASBJÖRNSEN, PETER CHRISTEN (Norwegian, 1812–1885)
MOE, JÖRGEN (Norwegian, 1813–1882)

Once there was a man who used to wander on foot through the picturesque villages and quaint little hamlets of Norway, talking to the peasants and gathering the fine old fairy tales of the people. This man was Peter Christen Asbjörnsen. When Peter was only fourteen years old he formed a firm friendship with a lad named Jörgen Moe. As the two grew to manhood, they found they were both interested in the same work, searching out their national fairy tales. They decided, therefore, to work together. Moe was a tutor, but in the holidays he, too, wandered through the mountains and into all sorts of out-of-the-way places, collecting tales and legends, and getting from many an old grandmother or simple minded maiden, some beautiful story to add to his collection.

In 1842 the first volume of their joint work appeared. It was called *Norwegian Popular Tales,* and was so well done that Asbjörsen and Moe have remained ever since the best known of all collectors of Norse Tales. Later, Asbjörnsen and Moe each did work alone, and Moe not only wrote fairy tales, but also some of the finest original and realistic stories ever written for children. Among the latter is the *Tale of Viggo and Beate,* which has been so beautifully translated by Gudrun Thorne-Thomsen in *The Birch and the Star.*

Important Works: Norwegian Popular Stories (translated by Sir George Dasent as Popular Tales from the Norse)

BACON, JOSEPHINE DODGE DASKAM (American, 1876–   )

EVEN while at Smith College, Josephine Dodge Daskam was noted for her cleverness and originality. Before she graduated, in 1898, she had had work published in the magazines. Mrs. Bacon has three children whose bringing up she considers the most important thing in her life. She loves children, gardening, making preserves, and raising pigs.

Important Works: Biography of a Baby; On Our Hill; The Imp and the Angel; Smith College Stories

BAILEY, CAROLINE SHERWIN (American, 1877–   )

Caroline Sherwin Bailey is a beloved kindergarten teacher of New York. She taught in the kindergartens of the public schools and at one time while engaged in this work, lived at the Warren Goddard Settlement in New York. Here she led story groups and studied the story needs of the children. For a long time she was editor of the Juvenile Department of the *Delineator.* Now she devotes her entire time to writing, lecturing and giving courses in story telling.

Important Works: Firelight Stores; For the Children's Hour; For the Story Teller; Stories Children Need; Tell Me Another Story

BARNUM, PHINEAS T. (American, 1810–1891)

On the fifth of July, 1810, heralded by a mighty thundering of cannon, a rattling of drums, and all the other noises of Independence Day, there appeared for the first time on this world's stage, a small boy, named Phineas T. Barnum, who was destined to become the greatest showman in all the world, and to make a bigger stir, both in America and Europe, than all the Independence Days put together. Phineas was born in the town of Bethel, Connecticut. His father was a tailor, a farmer and sometimes a tavern keeper, and Phineas led the life of an ordinary country boy, driving the cows to pasture, shelling corn, weeding the garden and riding the horse which led the ox team in ploughing. But the boy liked better to work with his head than with his hands, and he was always figuring out ways and means of earning money. On holidays, especially those days when the soldiers marched out and trained on the green with scores of country folk looking on, days when other boys were riotously spending all their hoarded pennies, Phineas was busy earning money! With bustling industry he peddled molasses candy, home-made gingerbread, cookies and sugar candies among the crowd, thus generally finding himself richer at the end of the holiday by many a merry penny.

As Phineas grew up he tried keeping a country store. A jolly place it was, where in the evenings and on rainy days, all

the wits and wags of the village gathered, to sit around the stove and talk or play jokes on one another, for all his life long Phineas dearly loved a joke. But keeping store was by no means in Phineas's line; he was only moderately successful and it was not until he was twenty-five years old, married and with a little daughter of his own, that he found the work for which he was really fitted. This work was nothing more or less than providing people with clean and wholesome amusement.

In 1835, Barnum heard of a remarkable negro woman named Joice Heth who was said to be one hundred and sixty-one years old and to have been the nurse of George Washington. She was a dried up, little, old creature, looking almost like a mummy, with a head of bushy, thick, grey hair. She lay stiff on a couch and could not move her limbs, nevertheless, she was pert and sociable, and would talk as long as anyone would converse with her. It was said that she had lain for years in an out-house on the estate of a certain John S. Bowling in Virginia, having been there so long that nobody knew or cared how old she was until one day Mr. Bowling accidently discovered an old bill of sale describing this woman as having been sold by Augustine Washington, father of George, to his half sister, Elizabeth Atwood. Being greatly interested in Joice, Barnum sold out his store for $500 and with this little capital, he started out to exhibit her.

He saw in the very beginning of his career that everything depended on getting the public excited and interested, to think and talk of what he had to exhibit. Accordingly, he made great use of advertisements in newspapers and every other means to arouse public interest. As a result, his showrooms in New York, Boston, Albany and elsewhere, were thronged, and he earned a vast return on his money. Joice would prattle away garrulously about her "dear little George," meaning George Washington, and she would tell how she had been present at the birth of the Father of His Country, and had been the one to put the very first clothes on the dear little infant. Often people would ask her questions about the Washington family and she would answer all, and was never caught in a single contradiction. When interest in the old woman appeared to flag, Barnum secretly caused the newspapers to agitate the question whether she was not, after all, a mere automaton and no living woman, a made image that talked and moved by means of machinery and springs. Then more crowds of people flocked to his hall to find out the truth about her.

Barnum's next venture after Joice Heth, was an Italian juggler who performed certain remarkable feats of balancing, plate spinning and stilt walking. This man called himself Signor Antonio and had once travelled with a monkey and a hand organ in Italy, but Barnum induced him first to take a bath and then to take upon himself the much more imposing name of Signor Vivalla. By dint of much advertising, he then made Vivalla very popular, and so remarkable was Barnum's ability to turn everything, even criticism, to good account, that he won his greatest success with Vivalla, by making good use of a hiss of derision that greeted one of the Signor's appearances from the audience. Far from being downcast by this hiss, Barnum sought out the one who had made the contemptuous noise and found him to be one, Roberts, a circus preformer, who insisted that he could do all Vivalla had done and more. Immediately Barnum challenged Roberts to hold a contest with Vivalla, offering a thousand dollars prize to the winner. He then advertised the trial of skill far and wide until he got the public interest at a white heat, thus drawing packed houses both for the first and following contests.

In April, 1836, Barnum contracted for himself and Vivalla to join Aaron Turner's Traveling Circus Co. Barnum, himself, was to act as ticket seller, secretary and treasurer. Mr. Turner was an old showman, but to Barnum this traveling and performing in canvas tents was altogether new. For centuries, in England, dwarfs, giants and wild men had been popular, and there had been shows of jugglers, performing horses, dancing bears, feats of horsemanship, acrobats, rope-dancers, etc. at fairs and elsewhere. Indeed, an ancient hand-illumined Anglo-Saxon manuscript shows an audience in an arena or ampitheatre built during the Roman occupation of Britain diverted by a musician, a dancer and a trained bear, while Shakespeare, in *Love's Labours Lost*, refers to a famous performing horse of his day. Rope-dancers threw somersaults over naked swords and men's heads in the days of Charles II, and Joseph Clark, the original "boneless man," appeared in the age of James II, while George Washington and his staff attended a circus performance in Philadelphia in 1780. But the regular tenting circus that travelled about with wagons had not come into being either in England or America until sometime between the years 1805 and 1830. At first, these circuses were very small and modest exhibitions, met only at fairs, and they performed only in the daytime, because no means had been discovered for lighting the tent at night. But when in 1830, the method of lighting the ring with candles in a frame around the center pole was devised, the circus began to grow. Turner's Circus, with which Barnum first travelled, was a moderate sized show and they set forth with quite a train of wagons, carriages, horses and ponies, a band of music and about twenty-five men. Their tour was very successful for all concerned, but in the fall Barnum took friendly leave of Turner and with several wagons, a small canvas tent and such performers as Vivalla, James Sandford, a negro singer and dancer, several musicians and Joe Pentland, one of the cleverest and most original of clowns, he began a little traveling exhibition of his own.

In Camden, South Carolina, Sandford suddenly deserted the company, and as Mr. Barnum had advertised negro songs at his performance, he was obliged to black his own face and hands, go on the stage and sing the advertised songs himself. To his surprise he was roundly applauded. But, when, in his negro black, he hurried out after one of these performances, to uphold some of his men against a white man who was abusing them, the fiery Southerner, taking him in truth for a negro, drew his pistol and shouted, "You black rascal, how dare you use such language to a white man!" Only the greatest presence of mind, which prompted Barnum to roll up his sleeve in a twinkling and reveal his own white skin, saved him from a bullet.

In going from Columbus, Georgia, to Montgomery, Alabama, Barnum's Company was obliged to cross a thinly settled, desolate tract known as the "Indian Nation," and as several persons had been murdered there by hostile Indians, it was deemed dangerous to travel the road without an escort. Only the day before the stage coach had been held up in that region. The circus men were all well armed, however, and trusted that their numbers would seem too formidable to be attacked, but they said quite openly that they earnestly wished there were no need to run the risk. Vivalla, alone, declared himself to be fearless and loudly boasted that he was ready to encounter fifty Indians and drive them all into the swamp. Accordingly, when the party had safely passed over the entire route to within fourteen miles of Montgomery, and were beyond the reach of danger, Joe Pentland, the clown, determined to test Vivalla's much boasted bravery. Pentland had secretly purchased an old Indian dress with a fringed hunting shirt and moccasins, and these he put on, after coloring his face with Spanish brown. Then, shouldering his musket, he followed Vivalla and his party, and approaching stealthily, he leaped into their midst with a terrific war whoop. Barnum and Vivalla's other companions were all in the secret and they instantly fled, leaving the doughty hero alone with the foe. Without more ado, Vivalla took to his heels and ran like a deer. Pentland followed him, yelling horribly and brandishing his gun. After running a full mile, the hero, out of breath and frightened nearly out of his wits, dropped on his knees before his pursuer and begged for his life. The Indian levelled his gun at his victim but soon seemed to relent and signified that Vivalla should turn his pockets inside out. This he did, handing over to Pentland a purse containing eleven dollars. The savage then marched Vivalla to an oak, and with his handkerchief tied him in the most approved Indian manner to the tree. After this, Pentland joined Barnum and the others and as soon as he had washed his face and changed his dress they all went to the rescue of Vivalla. The little Italian was overjoyed to see them coming, but the very moment that he was released he began to swagger about again, swearing that, after his companions had fled, the one Indian who had first attacked them had been reinforced by six more. He had defended himself stoutly, he said, but the superior force of the seven huge braves had at last compelled him to surrender! For a week the party pretended to believe Vivalla's big story, but at the end of that time they told him the truth and Joe Pentland showed him his purse, desiring to return it. Inwardly, Vivalla must have been deeply chagrined, but outwardly he flatly refused to believe the

story, and stubbornly said that he would not take back the eleven dollars, insisting that the money could not possibly be his, since his purse had been taken, not by one Indian, but by seven!

Now, at length, Barnum began to long earnestly for some more settled and worth while phase of the show business. It happened at just this time that the American Museum in New York City was for sale at a moderate price, for the reason that it had not been run for some time past so as to make any money. It was a fine collection of curiosities and Barnum determined to buy it, though the price, low as it was, was enormous in comparison with the small amount of capital which he had been able so far to lay by. He had the most eager confidence, however, that he could manage the museum so as to make it pay large returns, and he had the courage to stake all that he had on his own enterprise, wit and ability. Accordingly, he offered to pay down all he possessed and to make enough out of the museum to pay the rest within a set space of time, agreeing that if he could not do so, he should forfeit not only the museum, but the whole amount that he had thus far paid.

So he found himself, at last, in possession of a valuable and instructive, as well as amusing, collection, well worthy that he should devote to it all his wonderful energies. There were all sorts of rare beasts and remarkably trained animals, from performing dogs to performing fleas, these latter only to be seen with their tiny carriages and outfits, through a magnifying glass. There were giants, dwarfs, jugglers, ventriloquists, rope-dancers, gypsies, Albinos and remarkable mechanical figures. Mr. Barnum banished all the poor and vulgar things which so frequently disfigured other performances of this kind, and devoted himself, heart and soul, to giving the public the best and cleanest performance to be found for twenty-five cents anywhere in the city.

He had such a remarkable understanding of human nature, and so keen and merry a wit, that he was always able to startle the public attention and keep people thinking and talking about his performances. Once he employed a man to go very solemnly and lay down three bricks at certain distances apart in front of the museum, then to pass as solemnly with a fourth brick in his hand from one of the three to another, picking up each and exchanging it for the one he held in his hand. In no time at all the mysterious doings of the brick-man had attracted a huge crowd of curious humanity trying to find out what he could possibly be about, and when at the end of every hour, according to Barnum's directions, the man walked as though still intent upon this strange business of his, into the museum, quite a little crowd of the curious would march up to the ticket office and buy tickets just to enter the building and learn, if they could, the secret of his strange doings.

Not only could Barnum use his wit to attract people into the museum, but he also used the same wit on occasion to get them out again. Sometimes people would come and bring their luncheons and stay all day in the building, so crowding it that others who wished to come in, had to be turned away and their twenty-five cent pieces thus were lost to the coffers of the museum. Once, on St. Patrick's Day, a crowd of Irish people thronged the place, giving every evidence, one and all, of intending to remain until sundown. Beholding an eager crowd without, pressing to come in, and the ticket seller forced of necessity to refuse their quarters, Barnum attempted to induce one Irish lady with two children to leave the place by politely showing her an egress or way out of the building through a back door into a side street. But the lady haughtily remarked that she had her dinner and intended to stay all day. Desperate then, Barnum had a sign-painter paint on a large sign TO THE EGRESS. This he placed over the steps leading to the back door where the crowd must see it after they had once been around the whole building and seen all there was to see. Plunging down the stairs, they read TO THE EGRESS, and knowing not at all the meaning of the word, they shouted aloud,

"Sure that's some new kind of animal!" Eager to take in everything, they crowded out the door, only to find that this wonderful new curiosity was the back street!

Once, Barnum engaged a band of wild Indians from Iowa for the Museum. The party consisted of a number of large, noble savages, beautiful squaws and interesting papooses. The men gave war dances on the stage with a vigor and enthusiasm that delighted the audiences. Nevertheless, these wild Indians considered their dances as realities, and after their war dances it was dangerous to get in their way, for they went leaping and peering about behind the scenes as though in search of victims for their knives and tomahawks. Indeed, a rope fence had to be built at the front of the stage to make certain that they should not, some night, plunge down upon their audience after one of their rousing war dances. Finding the responsibility of thus protecting the public to be rather heavy, Mr. Barnum decided to ask them to change their bill by giving a wedding dance instead of a war dance. But the Indians took the wedding dance as seriously as they had the war dance. At the first afternoon performance, Mr. Barnum was informed that he was expected to provide a large new, red woolen blanket at a cost of ten dollars for the bridegroom to present to the father of the bride. He ordered the purchase made, but was considerably taken aback when he was told that he must have another new blanket for the evening's performance, as the old chief would on no account permit that his daughter should be approached with the wedding dance unless he had his blanket as a present. Mr. Barnum undertook to explain to the chief that no blanket was required since this was not a real wedding. The old savage, however, shrugged his shoulders and gave such a terrific "Ugh!" that Barnum was glad to make his peace by ordering another blanket. As they gave two performances a day he was out of pocket $120.00 for twelve wedding blankets that week!

At another time, Barnum had at the Museum some powerful

Indian chiefs who had come on a mission from the West to Washington. Some of these were fine, dignified, splendid types of the race, but one was a wiry little fellow known as Yellow Bear. He was a sly, treacherous, bloodthirsty savage, who had killed many whites as they traveled through the far west in early days. But now he was on a mission to the Great Father at Washington, seeking for presents and favors for his tribe, and he pretended to be exceedingly meek and humble, begging to be announced as the "great friend of the white man". He would fawn upon Mr. Barnum and try to convince him that he loved him dearly. In exhibiting these Indians on the stage, Mr. Barnum explained the names and character of each. When he came to Yellow Bear, he would pat him familiarly upon the shoulder which always caused the old hypocrite to give the most mawkish grin and stroke his arm lovingly. Then, knowing that Yellow Bear did not understand a word he said, and thought he was complimenting him, Mr. Barnum would say in the sweetest voice, "This little Indian, ladies and gentlemen, is Yellow Bear, chief of the Kiowas. He has killed, no doubt, scores of white persons and he is probably the meanest, blackest hearted rascal that lives in the far west." Here Mr. Barnum patted him sweetly on the head, and Yellow Bear, supposing that his introducer was sounding his praises, would smile and fawn upon him and stroke his arm while the other continued,

"If the bloodthirsty little villain understood what I was saying he would kill me in a moment, but as he thinks I am complimenting him, I can safely state the truth to you, that he is a lying, thieving, treacherous, murderous monster." Here Mr. Barnum gave him another patronizing pat on the head and Yellow Bear, with a final pleasant smile, bowed to the audience as much as to say that his introducer's words were quite true and he thanked him for the high praises so generously heaped upon him!

Giants and dwarfs were always a great feature of Mr. Barnum's establishment. At different times he had the celebrated dwarfs, General Tom Thumb, Lavinia and Minnie Warren, Commodore Nutt, and Admiral Dot. In the darkest days of the Civil War he took Commodore Nutt to Washington, and President Lincoln, sad and overburdened, left a cabinet meeting to come out for a moment's relief and joke with the little fellow. Mr. Barnum had also the famous Novia Scotia giantess, Anna Swan, and, early in his career, a French giant, named Monsieur Bihin, and the Arabian giant, Colonel Goshen. One day Bihin and Goshen had a terrific quarrel. The Arabian called the Frenchman "a Shanghai" and the Frenchman called the Arabian "a Nigger!" From words the two were eager to proceed to blows. Running to the collection of arms in the Museum, one seized the murderous looking club with which Captain Cook was said to have been killed, and the other snatched up a crusader's sword of tremendous size and weight. Everything seemed ready for hopeless tragedy, but once again Barnum's quick and ready wit saved the day. Rushing in between the two enormous and raging combatants, he cried:

"Look here! This is all right! If you want to fight each other, maiming and perhaps killing one or both of you, that is your affair, but my interest lies here. You are under engagement to me, and if the duel is to come off, I and the public have a right to participate. It must be duly advertised and must take place on our stage. No performance of yours would be a greater attraction!"

This proposition, apparently made with such earnestness, caused the two huge creatures to burst into laughter, after which dose of healthy humor, they were unable longer to retain their anger, but shook hands and quarreled no more.

The American Museum was now tremendously successful, and in the year 1849, Mr. Barnum left it under the management of others, while he attended to the enterprise, which of all other exhibitions in his life, he was most proud. This was the bringing over to America of the famous Swedish singer, Jenny Lind, the "Swedish nightingale," as she was called, an enterprise quite different in character from any other that Mr. Barnum had ever undertaken. But he made it, by his genius for awakening public interest, a never-to-be-forgotten success, and Jenny Lind was received everywhere throughout the United States and Cuba with almost riotous attention, while President Fillmore, General Scott, Daniel Webster, and many famous men delighted to pay her homage.

Barnum's well earned success had made him very rich, and the year before Jenny Lind came to America, he had built himself a beautiful home at Bridgeport, Connecticut, where he lived. This place he called Iranistan. The house was built in an elegant, airy, oriental style, with domes and slender minarets that looked, when seen by moonlight, like a fairy palace, taken bodily from some Moslem garden across the Bosphorous, and set down there by wizardry, amid such different surroundings. At Iranistan he lived with his dearly loved wife and daughters.

He was now a very public-spirited man, engaged in all sorts of activities valuable to Bridgeport, always expanding the city, making it more beautiful, and using his means unsparingly for the benefit of the town. He often encountered old fogies who opposed all progress because they had not his far reaching vision and could not see with him what would be for the final good of the city. But he always managed either to win them over or to get the obstacles they raised out of the way, so that the improvements he intended could be carried through, whether it were a new seaside park or a new bridge across the river. His chief interest was in East Bridgeport, which lay on the opposite side of the river from Bridgeport proper. From pure farm land he turned this region into a thriving city, with factories, shops, and houses, and he lent money on very generous terms to workmen who wished to build homes over there. But in order to make East Bridgeport still more prosperous, he once undertook to induce the Jerome Clock Company to move there with all its employees and their families. He was assured that this concern was a sound and flourishing one, but its officers deliberately deceived him. In the belief that he was signing notes which should make him responsible for a certain moderate amount of money that he was willing to risk to repay them for moving, he was tricked into signing notes for many, many times more than that amount, until, one day, he awoke to find that the Clock Company had failed and he himself was a ruined man, responsible for their miserable debts, to many times more than the amount of all his fortune. Thus, for a stranger concern, with the running of which he had had nothing to do, he had lost every penny and had, beside, a mountain of debts on his back. For all this, moreover, he had been in no way to blame, unless by too great generosity and too honest a faith in human nature. Iranistan had to be given up and even the American Museum likewise. But in the face of this, his first misfortune, Barnum spent not a moment in complaint, discouragement or self-pity, although petty enemies hounded him and many whom he had thought his good friends in his high fortunes now turned him a cold shoulder. He set to work at once to rebuild his fortunes, and rejoiced, instead of repining, because this affair had separated for him his real friends from those who had only fawned upon him for what they could get out of him.

Tom Thumb was one of his real friends who offered to help him in any way, and after moving his wife and daughters into humble quarters, Barnum set out to exhibit Tom Thumb for a second time in Europe. For four years now, he worked incessantly, exhibiting various curiosities and lecturing, sending every penny he could earn back home to pay up his debts. During this time, too, occurred a second misfortune, the burning of beautiful Iranistan to the ground. But Barnum never let anything turn him from his purpose and so, in 1860, he found himself at last free from debt and able to buy back once again his beloved American Museum. When he appeared on the stage of the Museum, and it was publicly announced that he was free of his troubles and once again Manager there, the public received him with the most tremendous shouts of applause, which showed clearly how they respected him, and how through his years of honest attempts to bring them happiness, he had endeared himself to them. Such a huge demonstration of affection nearly broke Barnum down. His voice faltered and tears came to his eyes as he thought what a magnificent conclusion this was to all the trials and struggles of the past four years.

Soon after Barnum entered again upon his duties at the Museum there came to him a most interesting man, usually known as Grizzly Adams, from the fact that he had captured a great many grizzly bears at the cost of fearful encounters and perils. He was emphatically a man of pluck and had been for many years a hunter and trapper in the Rockies and Sierra Nevada Mountains. He came to New York with his famous collection of California animals captured by himself. These consisted of twenty or thirty immense grizzlies, several wolves, buffalo, elk,

and Old Neptune, the greatest sea lion of the Pacific. They had come from California on a clipper ship, sailing around Cape Horn. Old Adams had patiently trained these animals, too, and at terrific cost, for although all of them were docile now with him, there was not one of them but at times would give him a sly hit, and some of the bears had struck him so many times with their fearful paws that they had broken his skull. Old Adams was dressed in a hunter's suit of buckskin trimmed with the skins and bordered with the hanging tails of small Rocky Mountain animals; his cap consisted of the skin of a wolf's head and shoulders, from which depended several tails, and under this his bushy hair and long, white beard appeared. In fact, the man was as much of a show as his beasts.

Barnum bought a half interest in Adams' menagerie and erected a canvas tent for him. On the morning of his opening, preceded by a band of music, the old man had a fine procession down Broadway and up the Bowery. At the head of a train of cages bearing his animals, he rode on a platform wagon, dressed in his hunting costume and holding two immense grizzly bears by chains, while he sat astride of one larger still, the famous General Fremont. It was General Fremont who had given Old Adams the last fatal blow on his head, although he had since become so docile that Adams had used him as a pack bear to carry his cooking and hunting apparatus, and had even ridden on his back for hundreds of miles through the mountains. The old man pluckily insisted on living for months and exhibiting his bears, in spite of his broken skull.

In 1861, Barnum heard of some white whales that had been seen in the lower St. Lawrence, and he set out at once to capture one. On a little island in the great river, inhabited by French Canadians, he engaged twenty four fishermen to capture for him two white whales alive and unharmed. Scores of these creatures could at all times be discovered by their spouting within sight of the island. The men made a V shaped pen in the water, leaving the broad end open. When a whale got into this pen at high water, the fishermen closed the entrance with their boats making a tremendous noise and splashing to keep the whale in until low tide. Then the huge creature was left high and dry with too little water to swim in and so was easily captured. A noose of stout rope was slipped over his tail and he was thus towed to a large box lined with seaweed and partially filled with salt water. When two of these creatures were captured, Barnum went back to New York, sending out word in all directions at what time the whales were to pass through various towns on the line. Thus he drew tremendous crowds to the train to see the creatures.

During the Civil War Barnum was too old to fight, but he sustained his part loyally at home, and in 1865 was elected to the Connecticut legislature. He soon discovered in Hartford that the rich railroad interests had long had undue influence with the legislature and were getting bills passed very advantageous to themselves, but wholly unfair and detrimental to the people. Being no politician, but an honest man, Barnum set himself at once to remedy this evil, defeat the railroad interests, and restore justice to the people. He was making a great speech to this effect in the legislature after weeks of determined work to line-up voters against the railroads, a speech intended as his crowning effort to induce the passage of bills that would defeat their unjust schemes when the following telegram was handed him.

"American Museum in flames. Its total destruction certain."

Barnum read the telegram containing this terrific news without a sign of discomposure. Then he laid it calmly and coolly on his desk and continued his speech, speaking so logically and eloquently that he carried his point and won the legislation against the railroads. It was not until this was accomplished that he made known the calamity which had befallen him and returned to New York. The destruction of the Museum was complete. In a breath had been wiped out the accumulated results of many years of incessant toil. Barnum had lost another fortune. Moreover, he was now fifty-five years old and might well have thought himself too old to start out life anew, but he did no such thing. He set about at once to establish a new American Museum, sending agents all over Europe and America to gather curiosities, and at the end of four months he had opened Barnum's New Museum.

Three years later, Mr. Barnum was sitting with his wife and a guest at breakfast one cold winter morning, and carelessly glancing over the newspaper when he suddenly read aloud, "Hallo! Barnum's Museum is burned!"

"Yes," said his wife, with an incredulous smile, "I suspect it is."

He had read the announcement so coolly and with so little excitement that his wife and friend did not believe it, and yet it was true. A third disastrous fire had wiped out his new museum. When he returned to New York he found its ruined walls all frozen over with water from the fire hose, the entire front with its ornamental lamp posts and sign one gorgeous framework of transparent ice, that glistened beautifully in the sun.

Now, at last, the celebrated showman decided to retire from active business and live on the remnant of his fortune. He tried hard to content himself with such a life of leisure, traveling about the United States, hunting buffalo with General Custer on the plains of Kansas, and for several years endeavoring in every way to amuse himself. But this experience only showed him that a life of inactivity was absolutely unendurable. He decided conclusively, once and for all, that the only true rest is to be found in useful activity, and by 1870 he had bigger plans than ever. He now determined to devote himself entirely to a great traveling circus, far larger and better than anything that had ever been done before. On this circus he labored unremittingly, confident that if he devoted his best energies to the public, the public would liberally repay him. Perceiving that his show was too gigantic to be moved in the old way by wagons he now for the first time arranged with railroads to transport it, using seventy freight cars, six passenger cars and three engines. The circus was a tremendous success. People crowded to the various places of exhibition, coming not only from the towns where the show was held, but from neighboring towns as well, some on excursion trains, and some by wagons or on horseback, often camping out over night.

Two years later, on the day before Christmas, Barnum was sitting at breakfast in a hotel, thinking comfortably how he had arranged for his circus to be shown in New York in order that his vast host of men should not be thrown out of employment during the winter, when once again a telegram was handed him saying that a fourth fire had completely destroyed this circus. This time Barnum had no thought of giving up again. He had decided beyond the shadow of a doubt that there were no real misfortunes in the world, and that what seemed even an overwhelming misfortune was only an opportunity for rising to greater accomplishments. Therefore he merely interrupted his breakfast long enough on this occasion to go out and send immediate cables to his European agents to duplicate all his animals within two months. He then went back and finished his meal. By the first of April he placed on the road a combination of curiosities and marvels far surpassing anything he had ever done before.

But great as this circus was, Barnum was never satisfied to rest on his laurels. He aimed to do something greater still. In 1874 while he still continued the traveling circus he opened in New York a great Roman Hippodrome. This gorgeous spectacle began every evening with a Congress of Nations, a grand procession of gilded chariots and triumphal cars, conveying Kings, Queens and Emperors, each surrounded by his respective retinue, and all in costumes made with the greatest care to be historically correct. This vast pageant contained nearly one thousand persons and several hundred horses, beside elephants, camels, llamas, ostriches, elands, zebras and reindeer. The rich and varied costumes, armor and trappings, gorgeous banners and paraphernalia, as well as the appropriate music accompanying the entrance of each nation, produced an effect at once brilliant and bewildering. The entire press said that never before since the days of the Caesars had there been so grand and interesting a public spectacle.

Most of Mr. Barnum's competitors in the circus field in those early days were men of very inferior aims and abilities, content with poor and inferior, even vulgar shows, aiming only to make money, and inspired with little of that desire to give in the biggest sense the best and finest entertainment possible, which made Mr. Barnum so different from the others. But in 1880 he found a rival worthy of his mettle in the person of Mr. James A. Bailey. The very moment that Mr. Barnum perceived Mr. Bailey to be a man with the same big aims and ambitions as himself, as well as the same solid business sense, far from feeling any jealousy and trying to drive him out of the field, he entered at once into negotiations with him and took him into partnership. This partnership with Bailey lasted throughout the remainder of Barnum's life. They opened their combined show with a street parade by night in New York, all beautifully illumined by calcium lights.

This huge circus now when it traveled had its own cars. No longer were the trains hired as of old from the railways. Advance agents and advertising cars, gorgeous with paint and gilding, containing paste vats, posters and a force of men, would pass through the country weeks ahead of the circus, pasting up the billboards and arousing the interest of the community. The circus itself was packed up in the smallest possible space, its men trained with military promptitude and precision to work like clockwork and make every move count in erecting or taking down the huge canvas city. The performers slept in their cars and ate in the canvas dining tent. Hundreds of men were employed and the expenses of the concern were four or five thousand dollars a day.

One of the most interesting feats of Barnum's later years was the purchase of Jumbo, the largest elephant ever seen. Jumbo was the chief ornament of the Zoological Gardens in London, and a great favorite with Queen Victoria whose children and grandchildren were among the thousands of British youngsters who had ridden on Jumbo's back. Mr. Barnum never supposed that Jumbo could be purchased, nevertheless he made a liberal offer for him to the Superintendent of the Gardens and his offer was accepted. When it became publicly known that Jumbo had been sold and was to depart for America, a great hue and cry was raised in England. Newspapers talked of Jumbo before all the news of the day and children wrote supplicating letters to the superintendent begging that he be retained. Nevertheless the superintendent persisted and Jumbo had to go.

When the day of his departure arrived there came a great tug-of-war. As the agents tried to remove Jumbo, Alice, another elephant who had been for sixteen years Jumbo's companion and was called in fun his "wife", grew so excited that her groans and trumpetings frightened all the other beasts in the Zoo who set up such howlings and roarings as were heard a mile away. Midst such a grievous farewell, Jumbo was led forth into the street. But when the great beast found himself in such unfamiliar surroundings there awoke in his breast that timidity which is so marked a feature of the elephant's character. He trumpeted with alarm and turned to reenter the garden only to find the gates of his paradise closed. Thereupon he straightway lay down on the pavement and would not budge an inch. His cries of fright sounded to the uninitiated like cries of grief and attracted a huge crowd of sympathizers, many of them in tears. Persuasion had no effect in inducing Jumbo to rise and force was not permitted, for Mr. Barnum always insisted strictly that his animals be governed by kindness, not by cruelty. And indeed it would have been a puzzle what force to apply to so huge a creature as Jumbo. In dismay Mr. Barnum's agent sent him the following cable; "Jumbo has lain down in the street and won't get up. What shall we do?" Barnum immediately replied, "Let him lie there a week if he wants to. It is the best advertisement in the world."

After twenty-four hours, however, the gates of the garden were reopened and Jumbo permitted to go in again. Barnum's agents now decided to take the huge beast in another way. A great cage on wheels was provided and moved up close to the door of Jumbo's den. When the elephant had been induced to enter the cage the door was closed and the cage was dragged by twenty horses to a waiting steamer where quarters had been prepared for Jumbo by cutting away one of the decks. Thus he was brought to America, and later Mr. Barnum acquired Alice likewise.

In 1884 Mr. Barnum got the rarest specimen of all his zoo, a royal sacred white elephant from Burmah. The animal was not pure white as had been supposed in Europe but was grayish. No European monarch had ever succeeded in getting one of these elephants into a Christian country for the Siamese and Burmese people believed that if a sacred white elephant left their country some dire misfortune would come upon them. Barnum's agents many months before had purchased a white elephant, but on the eve of its departure, its attendant priests gave it poison rather than permit it to fall into Christian hands. Finally, however, after three years of patient persistence, diplomacy and tact, as well as an outlay of a quarter of a million dollars, Barnum succeeded through his agents in getting from King Theebaw at Mandalay in Burmah, the sacred white elephant, Toung Taloung. He came to America in all his gorgeous trappings, accompanied by a Burmese orchestra and retinue of Buddhist priests in full ecclesiastical costume.

Mr. Barnum built for his great show enormous winter quarters at Bridgeport. A ten acre lot was enclosed and in this enclosure numerous buildings were constructed. There was an elephant house, kept heated at just the right temperature naturally required by these animals, where thirty or forty elephants could be luxuriously housed and trained; another building held lions, tigers and leopards, which require a different temperature, and still another housed camels and caged animals. The monkeys had roomy quarters all to themselves where they could roam about and work their mischievous will unrestrained. The hippopotami and sea-lions had a huge pond heated by steam pipes and here the elephants also were permitted their supreme enjoyment, a bath. There was a nursery department for the receipt and care of new-born animals, and in the various buildings many of the beasts were permitted to leave their cages and frolic at large.

In 1887, when Barnum was fast asleep in the middle of the night, a telegram arrived, stating that a fifth great fire had totally destroyed these splendid winter quarters. His wife awoke him at two o'clock in the morning and told him of the telegram.

"I am very sorry, my dear," he said calmly, "but apparent evils are often blessings in disguise. It is all right." And with that he rolled back into his original comfortable position and in three minutes was once again fast asleep.

Barnum was now seventy-seven years old, but with the help of his partner, Mr. Bailey, he rose as triumphant from this last fire as from all the others and soon had a better circus than ever. To the end of his days his energy, pluck and healthy ambition gave the people a better, completer and cleaner performance than has ever been given by any other showman. With his kindly face beaming, he often said, "To me there is no picture so beautiful as ten thousand smiling, bright-eyed, happy children, no music so sweet as their clear, ringing laughter. That I have had power, year after year, by providing innocent amusement for the little ones, to create such pictures, to evoke such music, is my proudest and happiest reflection."

BATES, CLARA DOTY (American, 1838–1895)

Mrs. Bates was a writer of stories and poems for children.

BENNETT, HENRY HOLCOMB (American, 1863–)

Mr. Bennett is known chiefly for his stories of frontier Army life.

BJÖRNSON, BJÖRNSTERNE (Norwegian, 1832–1910)

In the year 1832 a small boy was born in the rugged land of Norway. As he grew older the lad seemed a wild and unruly little fellow, and the forces at work within him as strong and untamed as the powerful sea that beat up on Norway's rock-bound coast. At school he was the despair of his tutors. Try as they would, they could never arouse in him the smallest interest in any of the regular studies. His parents even thought seriously of sending their son to sea in the hope that he might be tamed by the stern discipline of a sailor. But at last, with great difficulty, young Bjornson passed the entrance examinations for the University of Christiana, and there he suddenly found the line of activity to which he could devote all that bounding energy that had heretofore run away with him.

He discovered that at this time there was no national drama in Norway. Actors on the stage were giving light French comedies, or parading through the heavy action of some German play, or producing the latest Danish novelties from Copenhagen. At this miserable state of things young Björnson's patriotism took flame.

"Danish actors and plays must go!" he cried. "Let us have a real Norwegian drama!" And he set himself immediately to write Norwegian plays. But when the first fire of his patriotic wrath had cooled, he was forced to admit that at that time the Danish theatre was far superior to the Norwegian, and if he really wished to do something fine for Norwegian literature, he would have to swallow his pride and be willing to learn of Denmark. Accordingly, at the age of twenty four he set out for Copenhagen, there to study patiently all there was to learn. Henceforth, the boy whom tutors had been unable to drive to work that did not interest him, labored and worked without ceasing. His Norway should have a literature.

He wrote first a story called Synnöve Solbakken, which was

different from anything else that had ever been done in Norway. Heretofore it had been the fashion for Norwegian authors to write romantic tales of Italy or some other far-off land, but Björnson had the courage to seek his material right at home. He wrote about Norway and homely Norse peasant-life with an utter simplicity and freshness that were all his own. Never before had Norse peasant life been so sympathetically studied and so beautifully portrayed. Björnson's work became instantly popular.

On his return from Copenhagen, Björnson was made editor of The Norse People's Journal, but he also became director of the National Theatre in Bergen, and now at last, he began to publish in rapid succession a series of national dramas, the subjects of which were taken from the old Norse or Icelandic sagas. As in his novels he had aimed to bring into literature the type of the modern Norse peasant, so in his dramas he strove to present what was most thoroughly Norse out of Norway's historic past.

As time went on, a still more serious purpose took root in Björnson's heart. He was no longer satisfied with mere literary beauty in his work. It was no longer his ambition only to please and amuse. He began to see clearly the faults that existed in Norwegian society, and to wish to bring home to the Norwegian people some recognition of these faults and a real desire for reform. So now he spoke out plainly and depicted these faults in his dramas. Most particularly it was the oppression, injustice and cold conventionality of the upper classes as opposed to the modern workman's world that he so strikingly portrayed. Naturally, these plays of his cost him much of his popularity with "people of quality." Many a nobleman now turned him a decided cold shoulder. Nevertheless, such work revealed in him a still higher sense of patriotism than that of his earlier days, and a truer and far more unselfish devotion to the best interests of his people.

From now on, Björnson took a strong interest in the politics of his time. He proved an eloquent orator and wielded great influence in obtaining more liberal government. He believed wholeheartedly in a republic, but was opposed to the use of violent means to establish it in Norway. In 1880 he traveled through the United States, studying how a republic really works out in practice, and lecturing with great success to his countrymen in the West.

During the later years of his life Björnson was awarded the Noble prize for literature, the greatest honor which the world today can bestow upon an author. He has proved to be one of the greatest poets, dramatists and novelists that Norway has ever known, and in addition to this, he was the most Norwegian of all Norwegian writers.

BLAKE, WILLIAM (English, 1757–1827)

William Blake was the first English poet to express in his verse the thoughts and feelings of little children. Other poets had written of grown people, but Blake in his *Songs of Innocence* saw straight into the heart of the little child and for the first time uttered what was there in poetry. Blake was an engraver, too, and he decorated his poems with beautiful designs which were afterwards colored by hand. As he grew older, Blake lost the joyousness with which he had written *Songs of Innocence*, and wrote the sad and bitter *Songs of Experience*. Then, alas! men said he was mad, but his *Songs of Innocence* remain his loveliest work.

SONGS OF INNOCENCE
Little lamb, who made thee,
Dost thou know who made thee,
Gave thee life and bade thee feed,
By the stream and o'er the mead?

SONGS OF EXPERIENCE
Tiger, tiger, burning bright,
In the forests of the night,
What immortal hand or eye
Could frame thy fearful symmetry?

BROWN, ABBIE FARWELL (American, contemporary)

Abbie Farwell Brown was born in Boston and educated at Radcliffe College. She has traveled a great deal in Europe, is unmarried and has contributed many short stories to magazines.

The Lonesomest Doll *John of the Woods* *The Flower Princess* *The Christmas Angel*

THE LATCH KEY

BROWNE, FRANCES (Irish, 1816– ?)

HERE is the story of a little girl who was blind from the time she was eighteen months old, who never saw with her eyes the blue sky, the green trees, the fresh spring flowers, and yet found within herself a great, wide, beautiful, wonderful world which she saw far more vividly and could describe to others far more clearly than many who could see.

Frances Browne was born in the little mountain village of Donegal in Ireland, in the year 1816. She was the seventh of twelve children, and her father, the village postmaster, was in the poorest circumstances. Because she was blind, Frances was not given the education that was freely offered to her brothers and sisters, and by them so little valued; but with persistent determination she fought her way to that knowledge. Every evening she used to listen when her brothers and sisters recited their lessons aloud in preparation for the next day's classes, and would learn what they said by heart, untiringly reciting it to herself when everyone else was asleep, to impress it upon her memory. During the day, she would hire her brothers and sisters to read to her by promising to do their share of the household tasks in return. Thus, in exchange for numberless wipings and scrubbings in the kitchen, she received lessons in grammar, geography and various other subjects. Whenever her offer of doing their work failed to win her brothers and sisters, she would engage their services by repeating to them stories which they themselves had read and long ago forgotten, or by inventing for them the most interesting and fanciful tales of her own.

There were no book stores in Stranorlar or within three counties round about, nor were there any spare pennies at home with which to buy books. So Frances borrowed treasured volumes from all who came to the house and from everyone in the village. And thus as time passed, she acquired a better education than many a child who could see.

From the age of seven, Frances began to write poems, but when she was fourteen she heard the *Iliad* read and was so impressed with its grandeur, that her own poems seemed paltry things and in utter disgust she threw them into the fire. It was not until she was twenty-four years old that a volume of Irish songs was read to her and her own music thus reawakened. She now wrote several poems which were offered to various magazines, and to her great joy and astonishment, accepted and printed. After this, her work began to be successful and the first use to which she put her earnings was to educate a sister to read to her and be her secretary. In 1847 she set out for Edinburgh to begin her literary career, taking with her the sister-secretary and her mother, and assuming, blind though she was, the responsibility for supporting all three of them. In Edinburgh she wrote steadily anything she was asked to write, tales, sketches, reviews, poems, novels, and stories for children. Her industry was amazing, and though she never earned a great deal of money, she made friends with some of the greatest men and women of the day, and was always able to fulfill her affectionate purpose of caring for her mother.

Frances Browne's best loved works were her stories for children, and of these, the most popular was *Granny's Wonderful Chair* which was written in 1856. For many years this interesting book was out of print, but in 1887 Frances Hodgson Burnett republished it with a preface, under the title *Stories From the Lost Fairy Book, retold by the child who read them.* Since then, *Granny's Wonderful Chair* has returned to its rightful place in children's literature.

How wonderful was the richness of that world which this blind girl found within her own darkness! Nowhere in all her works is there a word of complaint about her blindness; there is only the giving forth of a wealth of joy and beauty. How did a writer who never saw a coach or a palace, or a picture of a coach or a palace, tell so convincingly of coaches and palaces and multi-

tudes? Whence came her vivid word-pictures of the little cottage on the edge of a great forest with tall trees behind, the swallows building in the eaves, the daisies growing thick before the door? A love of nature was in her soul. In spite of her blindness she found within herself a wonderful perception of the beauty of the world. With her poet's spirit she saw all the green and leafy places of the earth, all its flowery ways—while these were trodden heedlessly, mayhap, by those about her with the gift of sight. It was amazing, too, the wonderful reach of her knowledge—her stories are of many lands and many periods, from the French Revolution and the scenery of Lower Normandy, to the time of the Young Pretender in England; from the fine frosts and clear sky, the long winter nights and long summer days of Archangel, to the banks of the Orange River in Africa. And she was perfectly at home, whether she told of shepherds on the moorland, the green pastures dotted with snow white sheep, or whether her fancy dived beneath the sea midst hills of marble and rocks of spa.

Indeed, the story of Frances Browne's life is scarcely less interesting than her own wonderful books of fancy, and there has never been a nobler example of the fact that circumstances can never conquer a strong and beautiful spirit. She who in poverty and blindness could secure her own education and press on through every obstacle to the most complete development of her powers, giving to the world a wealth of joy and beauty, and never a word of complaint, has indeed left in her own life as beautiful a story as could ever be written.

Important Works: Granny's Wonderful Chair.

BROWNING, ELIZABETH BARRETT (English, 1806–1861)
BROWNING, ROBERT (English, 1812–1889)

In a most picturesque and lovely home in the Malvern Hills, near Wales, there lived once with ten lively brothers and sisters, a little girl named Elizabeth Barrett. The country round about that fine old place was wonderfully green and beautiful;

Dimpled close with hill and valley,
Dappled very close with shade;
Summer snow of apple blossoms
Running up from glade to glade.

And the little girl drank in the loveliness of it all as she raced and chased and romped about with her brothers and sisters. She was very fond of books, too, and when her best beloved brother, Edward, began to study Greek with a tutor, she joined him and used to sit in her little chair with her book in one hand and a doll tenderly cherished in the other, persistently twisting her tongue around the strange Greek words. Ever after, Elizabeth continued to love the old Greek stories and to study them. Sometimes she said that she dreamed more often of Agamemnon than of Moses, her beautiful black pony. One year the little girl had a great flower bed laid out in the garden. It was shaped like an enormous giant. This, she said, was Hector, son of Priam, mighty hero of Troy. He had eyes of blue gentians and scented grass for locks; his helmet was made of golden daffodils, his breastplate of daisies, and in his hand, all ready for the fray, he bore a sword of lilies.

Elizabeth's very closest chum in her childhood was her father, a fine type of English gentleman. Often she used to write little poems and show them to him in secret, when no one else was about.

But when she was fourteen years old she wrote a long poem of fifteen hundred lines, all about one of the Greek stories she loved. It was called "The Battle of Marathon," and her father thought it so remarkable that he had it published.

The girl was a wonderfully graceful, dainty little creature, of a slight, delicate figure, with a shower of dark curls falling on either side of a most expressive face. Her eyes were large and tender, richly fringed by dark lashes, and her smile was like a sunbeam.

One day, when she was fifteen, Elizabeth decided to go for a ride on her pony, Moses. But Moses was not brought up, ready and harnessed, exactly on the moment when she wanted him, so, in a fit of impatience she flounced out after him into the field. There she attempted to saddle him herself, but as she did so, she fell and the saddle came crashing down on top of her. The result of her impatience was that she was severely hurt, and there followed for her years of invalidism, during which she never went out again in the same old free way, to ramble over the hills and romp in the out-of-doors.

As time passed she went to live in various different places, for a while in Torquay in beautiful Devonshire, but wherever she went there hung over her almost continuously this cloud of illness. The long days when she was confined to her room she spent in study and in writing poetry for various magazines, but for many years her chief means of communication with the outside world was by means of letters only. Nevertheless, these letters of hers were always bright and vivacious with small mention of her troubles. Little by little, the young woman, thus so constantly confined to a sick room, grew to be a well known poet. It is noteworthy, too, that the poems she wrote under such conditions had no hint of weakness, but were rather remarkable for their strength.

One day a great man, one of the greatest of English poets, wrote Elizabeth Barrett a letter in admiration for her work. This great man was Robert Browning, and Elizabeth Barrett admired

Robert Browning: The Pied Piper of Hamlin. An Incident of the French Camp.

his work as much as he did hers, so that they soon began writing regularly to one another. The outcome of their correspondence was that Mr. Browning came one day to see the delicate little lady and induced her to marry him, although she thought herself too weak and ill to marry anyone. Her new joy and happiness, however, lifted her out of her invalidism and almost transformed her. Mr. Browning carried her off with him to live beneath the warm and sunny skies of Italy and here the two spent all the rest of Mrs. Browning's life. It was chiefly in the interesting old town of Florence, with its hoary, gray stone buildings and its splendid treasures of art, that they lived. Mrs. Browning took the keenest interest in the Italian people who were just then struggling for their independence, and as she looked down on the ardent young patriots from the windows of her home, the famous Casa Guidi palace, she wrote poems full of love and sympathy for them. Indeed, her poetry is always full of the deepest and tenderest feeling and the truest love for all that is just and good.

It was in Florence, too, that a little son, Robert, was born to Mrs. Browning, and the mother, who by now had become the greatest of living women-poets, had as much joy in all the wonderful things her little boy did as any less famous mother.

The life of Elizabeth Barrett and Robert Browning was remarkably happy together. They visited Venice and all the most beautiful spots in Italy and were absolutely one in the love, admiration and devotion which they bore to one another. Frequently they were visited by friends, many of whom were Americans, and whoever was fortunate enough to be the guest of the Brownings in their happy home, always came away deeply impressed with the beautiful family life he had seen there.

When Mrs. Browning died, the citizens of Florence, grateful for her love and sympathetic understanding, placed on the wall of Casa Guidi a marble tablet sacred to her memory. Mr. Browning and his little son then went sorrowfully back to England.

Elizabeth Barrett Browning: Casa Guidi Windows; Aurora Leigh.

BRYANT, WILLIAM CULLEN (American, 1794–1878)

One of the descendants of that arch little Puritan maiden, Priscilla Mullins, and her bashful lover, John Alden, was a small boy named William Cullen Bryant. William was born in the beautiful hilly country of Cummington, Massachusetts, fit cradle for a real poet of Nature. His father, Dr. Peter Bryant, was a country physician, and he used to love to wander with his sons out into the wild woodlands and up into the hills, keen-eyed and alert to each flash of little woodland creatures through the leaves, loving them all and lifting up his heart with joy for all Nature's ways of beauty. Dr. Bryant was a lover of the English poets, too, and even used sometimes to write verses of his own. In the long winter nights, when the snow lay white on the world without and a roaring fire blazed on the cosy hearth within, he would often read aloud to his children from the treasures of his library which was one of the largest in the neighborhood. During the day the boys went to the public school, but when the school hours were over they raced out into the woods and fields, exploring all the country round about.

It was their habit, too, on these delightful rambles, to recite aloud to an audience of tall trees, scurrying rabbits, or even stones, the verses which they had been reading at home. Cullen particularly delighted in this happy custom, and often on his walks he composed and recited little poems of his own. One of these early verses he delivered in his school room, in his eleventh year, and it was afterwards published in the county newspaper, The Hampshire Gazette. The subject chosen for his poem by this ambitious youngster of eleven was, "The Advance of Knowledge."

When Cullen grew to young manhood he was sent to Williams College, but his father was too poor to permit him to finish his education at Yale University, as he had hoped, and so for a time he pursued his studies at home. It was at this period, when he was still little more than a youth, that, as he was one day wandering in the tangled depths of the rich primeval forest, his meditations framed themselves into that beautiful poem, *Thanatopsis*.

To him who in the love of nature holds
Communion with her visible forms, she speaks
A various language; for his gayer hours
She has a voice of gladness, and a smile
And eloquence of beauty; and she glides
Into his darker musings with a mild
And healing sympathy, that steals away
Their sharpness ere he is aware.

Having written the poem down on paper he laid it aside and appears to have forgotten it altogether. It was not until some six years later that his father accidentally discovered it, took it to Boston and had it published. It produced a decided impression at once, for no American poet had yet written anything to equal it.

From this time forth, though Cullen had been educated for a lawyer, he continued to devote himself to literature. In 1825, he became editor-in-chief and part proprietor of the New York Evening Post, a position which he held for fifty years. During all that time, by means of his articles in the Post, he helped to direct the current of national thought into the wisest and best channels. These important articles he had a habit of scribbling down on old envelopes and scraps of waste paper of which he always hoarded a generous store. The sincerity and earnestness with which he presented his principles and his quick native sense of justice, as well as his complete independence of all managing politicians, soon made of his paper a great power in the land.

When the question of the abolition of slavery began to be agitated, Bryant in the Post, took the side of the Abolitionists. This stand was decidedly unpopular in those days and brought down upon it a storm of abuse. The Post then began to lose favor with the public and it was only by the most persistent struggles that Bryant kept it alive against the tense and growing prejudices of the community. Mr. Bryant, however, refused to surrender a single one of his convictions, although he was denounced and deserted by many of his former friends, and was more than once threatened by the violence of the mob.

In 1860 he was one of the presidential electors who chose President Lincoln, and ever afterward he enjoyed the confidence and friendship of Lincoln. During the dark days of the Civil War, when all too many deserted and betrayed that gaunt, lone figure in the President's chair, Bryant stood firmly by him, ever aiding and supporting him, and no other journal was more instrumental than the Post in bringing about the great changes of public opinion which ended in the destruction of slavery.

Thus, the middle years of Bryant's life were too busy with hard work to leave much time for poetry. But when the years of national storm and stress were ended, he undertook his most ambitious literary work—translations of the *Odyssey* and the *Iliad.*

Mr. Bryant lived to be a very old man. He was the first American poet to win permanent distinction and he exercised a mighty influence over the younger literary men of America.

Important Works: Thanatopsis The Fountain To a Waterfowl

BURGESS, GELETT (American, 1868–)

Gelett Burgess was born in Boston. He was a draughtsman and instructor in topographical drawing at the University of California, but he is known chiefly as the author and illustrator of several whimsical books for children.

Important Works: The Lively City o' Ligg Goops and How To Be Them

BURGESS, THORNTON (American, 1874–)

THORNTON BURGESS was born in Sandwich, Massachusetts, and spent all his boyhood in the fields, the woods and marshes around this Cape Cod Town. Here he hunted, fished and made acquaintance with all the animals and birds. For some time he wrote nature articles for various magazines under the name of W. B. Thornton, but in all his spare moments he was out of doors, walking or boating, and studying wild life. At length he was made one of the editors of *Good Housekeeping* and it was in that magazine that he first won his name as a story teller for children.

His fascinating tales were first told to his own children, and for all that Peter Rabbit, Reddy Fox, and all the rest frisk through his stories in little coats and vests, trousers and hats, their habits are nevertheless as accurately true to the life of each animal as though his books were scientific nature studies.

Important Works: The Adventures of Peter Cottontail The Burgess Bird Book

BURNS, ROBERT (Scotch, 1759–1796)

IN a tiny, one-room, mud cottage near the village of Ayr in Scotland was born little Robert Burns. The boy's good father had built the hut with his very own hands, but its walls were so frail that only a week after the little fellow's birth, when there came up a violent gale, the house was blown into ruins. In the dead of night, mother and child were carried to a neighbor's dwelling for shelter.

A sturdy farmer was Mr. Burns and he meant his children to have an education. Accordingly, he and four of his neighbors hired John Murdoch to keep a school for their bairns and this kindly Scotsman lived in turn for a few weeks at a time with each of the different families. Little Robert, it is true, liked to play truant. He loved each "wee, modest, crimson-tipped flower," each "cowerin', timorous beastie" of the field, and the "sweet warbling woodlark on the tender spray" far better than his lessons. He loved, too, the "wild, mossy mountains," where grouse led their coveys through the heather and shepherds piped while they tended their sheep. Nevertheless, with infinite patience, Murdoch overcame the boy's truancy and won him to his studies.

Now there was at this time in the Burns' household an old woman named Betty Davidson, who knew more tales than anyone else in the country concerning fairies, ghosts and devils. In the eerie dusk of the cottage firelight, Robert sat at old Betty's knee and soaked in stories of witches and warlocks, of wrinkled beldames and withered hags, which were later to make a riot of fun through his poem of *Tam o' Shanter*. His mother, too, taught him the early romances and history of Scotland, arousing in his breast the deepest tenderness for his country. Many a time the little fellow was to be seen strutting down the village street in the wake of the drums and the squealing bagpipes. Later, while he followed the plough through the fresh-turned fields, he always had a book of ballads held up before him, and when the village blacksmith gave him a life of William Wallace to read, off he must go on the very first fine summer's day to explore every den and dell in Leglen Woods where Wallace was said to have hidden.

When Robert was fifteen years old, he worked once in the golden glowing harvest field by the side of a lassie who sang like a bird for sweetness. The sight and sound awoke in his heart the gift of song and called forth from him his first poem.

A sturdy, tender, affectionate lad was Robert Burns, but when he grew to be a youth he was sent to the country dancing school, and there he fell in with evil companions. Later, too, he met certain smugglers who plied their trade in the deep-hidden caves of the bare and rocky Ayrshire coast, and was attracted by their lawless ways and speech. He began to frequent the taverns, to drink and join in many a riotous revel. And so the poor lad's life could go but from bad to worse. His father died leaving a burden of debts; the farm was poor, crops failed and Robert found himself, at last, tangled and fast-bound in a host of difficulties. The only way out seemed to be for him to leave his country for far-off Jamaica.

In order to raise the passage money of nine pounds to take him to Jamaica, friends urged Burns to publish the poems which he had so long been writing. And thus appeared his first volume of verse. It was instantly praised and Burns at once became popular. Instead of going to Jamaica, he went to Edinburgh. From the little farm in Ayrshire he made his way to the fine old city which towered up proudly before him from Holyrood to the Castle, picturesque and smoke-wreathed by day, by night a climbing tier of lights and cressets. In Edinburgh he suddenly found himself a lion, feted and praised by all.

But alas! success in the city was short-lived. Burns recognized very shortly that he was wholly out of sympathy with the standards of the world. His downright honesty could not endure to bow and scrape before men of high rank who had no abilities whatsoever. How could he, whose heart was yearning to pay honor to whom honor was due, endure to meet at a great man's table Squire Somebody or Something, and see a fellow whose abilities would scarcely have made an eight-penny tailor and whose heart was not worth three farthings, meet with all the fawning notice and attention which were withheld from a man of genius, merely because he was poor? This was a state of affairs never to be endured by the man who could write:

Is there for honest poverty
That hangs his head and a' that?
The cowara slave, we pass him by,
We dare be poor for a' that!
For a' that and a' that,
Our toils obscure and a' that,
The rank is but the guinea stamp;
The man's the gold for a' that!

What though on hamely fare we dine,
Wear hodden-grey and a' that;
Gie fools their silks and knaves their wine,
A man's a man for a' that.
For a' that and a' that,
Their tinsel show and a' that;
The honest man, though e'er sae poor,
Is King o' men for a' that.

Ye see yon birkie called a lord,
Wha struts and stares and a' that;
Though hundreds worship at his word,
He's but a coof for a' that.
For a' that and a' that,
His ribband, star, and a' that,
The man of independent mind,
He looks and laughs at a' that.

In the very heyday of his success in Edinburgh, Burns began to see that he should have to return to the country, don his "hodden-grey" once again and follow the plough. Accordingly, he turned his back on the city and married a country girl. Then he settled down to a small farm at Ellisland, with high hopes that here he should be happy. But poor Burns! In spite of his warm heart and

love of laughter, he was too weak and yielded too easily to temptation ever to be happy. The taverns and ale-houses saw him far too frequently again. How then could he make Ellisland pay? In a short time he had to sell it. With his wife and children he moved into the little town of Dumfries. And now he was separated from all that rustic country life and picturesque, rural scenery that had been his inspiration. He turned down no more daisies in the field; the horned moon hung no longer in his window pane; he saw no more rosebuds in the morning dew, so pure among their leaves so green. Amid the dirty streets, the gossip and dissipation of a third-rate Scottish town, he was neither in harmony with himself nor with the world. And so, at the age of thirty-one, worn out and old before his time, the greatest poet of Scotland died.

Robert Burns' songs came to him as naturally as the carol to the blackbird. In one short summer's day he dashed off all of *Tam o' Shanter*. His songs are full of laughter, full of tears and so immensely tender. In his heart was a great sympathy which reached out to all mankind, and to beasts and flowers of the field as well. He makes us smell the new-turned earth, the breath of kine, and the milk-white thorn that scents the evening gale, and yet his deepest interest was in men—in men and women, lads and lassies. First and foremost he was the poet of the fireside and the hearth, of the wee white cottage glinting through the trees, with smoke slow curling from its peaceful ingle-nook, where wait some thrifty wife and wee, sweet bairns to welcome home their Dad. His touch falls on men's souls like the touch of tender hands and of all great men from the North Country there is none who holds in his countrymen's hearts a place like Robert Burns.

Important Works: Tam O'Shanter — *To a Mountain Daisy*
The Cotter's Saturday Night — *For a' That and a' That*

BURROUGHS, JOHN (American, 1837–1921)

John Burroughs, the beloved student of woodsman's lore, was born in Roxbury, New York, and from his childhood always loved the woods and fields. Hidden away in the hills, in the infinite quiet and seclusion of the woods, he built the home called Slabsides and there, for many years he lived, while his admirers and friends made loving pilgrimages there to see him.

Important Works: Wake Robin Fresh Fields Winter Sunshine Signs and Seasons

BYNNER, WITTER (American, 1881–)

Witter Bynner is one of the most modern of American poets, conspicuous as a writer of free verse. He was graduated from Harvard in 1902 and became assistant editor of *McClure's Magazine*. Later he was instructor in English in the University of California, and has spent a year in China collecting Chinese poetry.

BYRON, GEORGE GORDON, LORD (English, 1788–1824)

A STORMY life was that of the handsome little Lord Byron, who at ten years of age inherited the estate and title of his great-uncle. Shy and lonely he was, fond of solitude, yet capable, too, of the fieriest attachments. He loved animals, but of the ferocious kind. A bear, a wolf and a bull dog were his pets at different periods. Lord Byron was lame from his birth and yet he took many a prize as a sportsman. He excelled particularly in swimming, and once, like Leander, swam across the Hellespont.

So headstrong was young Lord Byron that his whole life was darkened by his own ungoverned passions. His restlessness often drove him to travel and he described his travels in Europe in the poem *Childe Harold* which made him famous. Having wasted his youth, Byron determined to redeem himself in 1823 by going to help the Greek people, who were struggling to free themselves from the outrageous rule of the Turks, but while he still labored for the Greeks he was taken ill and died.

Important Works: Childe Harold

CARMAN, BLISS (Canadian, 1861-)

Bliss Carman was born at Fredericton, New Brunswick. At a meeting of Canadian authors in 1921, he was crowned with a wreath of maple leaves as the most distinguished poet of Canada.

Important Works: Songs from Vagabondia

CARROLL, LEWIS (CHARLES LUTWIDGE DODGSON) 1832–1898

Once there was a man and he was born in Cheshire, the county made famous as being the home of the grinning Cheshire cat! He was a lecturer on mathematics at Oxford University and wrote very deep and learned books with such awful sounding names as *Mathematica Curiosa*. But sometimes, this same most learned professor used to go out on golden afternoons in a boat with three little girls. The little girls would make believe that they could row the boat and busily pretend to guide its wanderings down the placid stream. Then they would all talk at once and beg the professor to tell them a story, and order him to put in lots of nonsense and fun and plenty of wild and new adventures! So the professor forgot that he was a professor and began to tell them a tale. O, such a tale as he told! While *Mathematica Curiosa* is long ago forgot, the story that he spun out on those golden afternoons, drifting down the dreamy river, with three little girls telling him just what to do and interrupting him every minute, that is the story that made him famous—*Alice in Wonderland*.

CATHER, KATHERINE DUNLAP (American, contemporary)

Katherine Dunlap Cather was born in Navarre, Ohio. She taught school in various places in California and did newspaper work in San Jose and San Francisco, always uniting with these activities much public work in story-telling. For years she has been a favorite contributor to *St. Nicholas* and other magazines.

Important Works: Educating by Story Telling. Boyhoods of Famous Men

CAWEIN, MADISON JULIUS (American, 1865–1914)

A writer of exquisite nature poetry, born in Kentucky.

CERVANTES, MIGUEL de (Spanish, 1547–1616)

A quaint, little old market place in a little old town in Spain and a crowd of simple folk gaping about a band of strolling players. There sat young Miguel and watched them, open mouthed with interest. A blanket hung over two ropes in the open square formed the sole decoration of this theatre and the actors went through the performance wearing worn old beards and wigs and clad in naught more elegant than white sheepskin dresses trimmed with gilt leather. Crude! And yet Miguel drank it all in, and the verses of those comedies remained fixed in his memory. Sometimes the young fellow took a hand himself at writing verses, but he liked adventure best and longed to be up and doing.

As soon as the opportunity offered, Miguel left Spain and was off to Rome to become a page in the household of an envoy of the Pope. But the life of a page, bowing and scraping, was intolerably slow and ineventful so he soon resigned his post and enlisted as a soldier in a Spanish regiment in Italy.

At this time Pope Pius V was organizing a Holy League against the Turks, whose barbarous conquests and inroads into Europe were alarming all Christendom. This league consisted of the Pope, Venice and Spain, and their forces were to be commanded by the famous Don John of Austria, a brilliant general who was half brother to King Philip II of Spain. The fleet of these three states was the largest that had ever sailed under a Christian flag. It consisted of galleys rowed by a large number of criminals under sentence. In the Turkish fleet the oarsmen were all Christian slaves. The object of the allies was to recover the island of Cyprus from the Turks. But before they had sailed so far they fell in with the enemy, and fought in the Gulf of Lepanto.

Miguel de Cervantes was acting only as a common soldier aboard one of the Christian galleys on that great day, but he behaved with conspicuous heroism. He placed himself at the head of a dozen men and took a position exposed to the hottest fire of the enemy. From here he boarded one of the Turkish galleys and engaged in a hand to hand conflict with the fierce and barbarous foe. In the course of the battle he received three gunshot wounds, two in his breast and one shattering his left hand, which was maimed for the rest of his life, but his conduct won for him the applause of all his comrades. The Christian fleet was victorious. One hundred and seventy Turkish galleys were captured and 15,000 Christian galley slaves set free.

A great storm followed this mighty victory, and Don John sailed away with his wounded men to Messina. Here Cervantes was given a special grant of money for his distinguished services, but so eager was he to be at the front again, that as soon as his wounds were healed, off he went to rejoin Don John. A second attempt to destroy the Turkish fleet, however, met sorry defeat and was followed by a long campaign in Africa. Cervantes and his comrades at last took the city of Tunis whose white walls had so long defied them. But alas! they held Tunis for only a very short time. Soon the Turks recaptured it and came swarming in again.

Thus passed four long years of struggle, during which time Cervantes had known all the hardships of war, the joys of victory and the sorrows of defeat. Having been away from home six years, and finding himself now worn and wounded in his country's service, he at length asked leave to return to his native land. This permission was granted him and he left Naples on a galley called El Sol, bearing letters from Don John to the King, in which Don John recommended him as "a man of valor, of merit and of signal services." But just as Cervantes, and his brother, Rodrigo, who was his companion, were rejoicing at sight of the Spanish coast which lay glistening before them and smiling a welcome home, there bore down upon them suddenly a squadron of Turkish pirates under a hideous captain who was the terror of the Mediterranean. Then followed a desperate fight, but the pirate galleys were too strong. Cervantes and a number of Spanish comrades were cap-

tured and carried off to Africa. There they found themselves placed at the mercy of a savage Greek who was noted for wild ferocity. As letters were found on Cervantes from Don John of Austria, he was believed to be a prize of great value, for whom a large ransom might be demanded. Heavily loaded with chains, he was sent off to Algiers, which, for centuries, was the stronghold of the fierce Algerian pirates. The city climbed, tier above tier, in gleaming white stone up the hillside from the coast, to be crowned by an ancient fortress, and there amid the narrow, dirty streets, the rich, heavily scented Oriental bazaars, Cervantes was held for five years a prisoner, subject to every caprice of his conqueror, and treated with sternest severity.

During his captivity, however, the sturdy Spaniard never once lost his courage nor his gay and cheerful humor. Adversity brought out the finest qualities of his character. Persistently and with great ingenuity he organized plans of escape, the failure of one plan never deterring him from setting to work at once to prepare another. On one occasion he even succeeded in getting himself and a party of comrades out of the city, but at the critical moment, a Moor who had been engaged to act as their guide, treacherously deserted them. The fugitives were obliged to return to Algiers and Cervantes was severely punished. The next year a sum of money was sent over by the parents of Cervantes, but it was not sufficient to induce the corsairs to release him. Instead, they let his brother, Rodrigo, go. Rodrigo set out for home with secret instructions to request that a war vessel be sent from Spain to rescue the others. Cervantes himself set about at once making all necessary arrangements to escape on this vessel. He gathered together about fifty Spanish fugitives and concealed them in a cave outside the city, actually managing to have them supplied with food for six months while they waited. At last, after these long months of patient endurance, the day came when the ship was to be expected. Cervantes and his comrades were in readiness to board her at once. But, just when freedom seemed so certainly in sight, a traitor once again betrayed their secret to the pirates. A force of armed Turks discovered their hiding place and captured them. Cervantes immediately took on himself all the blame for their scheme of flight, declaring that he, alone, was responsible. Though he was threatened with torture and even death, he refused to implicate any one of his comrades. The terrible governor, Hassan Pasha, before whom Cervantes was brought, was a monster of cruelty and did not hesitate, as a rule, to hang, impale or mutilate his prisoners, but on this occasion he was overawed by Cervantes' astounding fearlessness, and did little more than threaten.

Still a third and fourth plan of escape were devised. At last, two merchants agreed to provide an armed vessel in which sixty captives were to embark. This ship lay ready at hand when a Spanish monk, who hated Cervantes, revealed the plan to the Turks. Cervantes, himself, might have escaped even then, if he had gone off at once with the merchants and left his comrades behind. But nothing could induce him to desert his companions in distress. Instead, he came forward once more and gave himself up to the Governor. He was bound and led with a rope around his neck before Hassan. This time he fully expected to be hanged, or, at least, to have his nose and ears cut off, and, indeed, what would have happened to Cervantes had not Hassan still hoped to obtain a high ransom for him, no one can tell. As it was, he condemned him to five months' close confinement in chains.

At last, at the end of five years, friends and relatives in Spain raised sufficient ransom money to set the captives free. And thus, after eleven long years' absence, Cervantes made his way home. He reached Spain to find his family impoverished, his patron, Don John of Austria, dead, and no one to speak a good word for him to the haughty and selfish King Philip II. Spain at this time, in 1580, was at the very height of her power, dominating the world by land and sea, wringing gold, gold, gold from her people at home and bearing it in great treasure ships from her distant colonies in Mexico and Peru. Imperial ambition and the worship of force were the keynotes to Philip's character, and he had little time to waste thought on a worn-out soldier like Cervantes. What heartaches were in store in Spain for the gallant Spaniard! His services, his work, his sufferings were all forgotten—and yet from these trials also he emerged sweetened and strengthened, still in possession of his gay courage and his dauntless good humor.

In the most straitened circumstances, he married and settled down, and now there was naught to do, but to take up once more his old pastime of writing. The most popular Spanish writer of the day was one Lope de Vega. He wrote plays by the score and was rich and honored, with many powerful friends, while Cervantes had no friends and no crumb of royal favor. In face of these disadvantages, and struggling against poverty, he wrote his greatest work, *Don Quixote.* No sooner did this book appear in 1605, than behold! it found instant favor with the people. But literary men criticized it, and Lope de Vega, from his height of superiority, wrote, "No poet is so bad as Cervantes nor so foolish as to praise *Don Quixote.*"

The books people read in those days were mostly romances of chivalry, recording the absurd adventures of wonderful knights-errant who wandered about rescuing captive princesses from castles and performing miraculous deeds of prowess, all written quite seriously. Cervantes, with his knowledge of life as it really was, wished to ridicule this sort of literature and show up its absurdity. That is what he did in *Don Quixote,* but so fertile was his imagination and so varied had been his own experiences, that at the same time he succeeded in getting into his book a wonderfully graphic picture of Spanish life in his day, bringing in all classes of society, and also recounting many of his own adventures as a soldier. Moreover, the broad humanity he had learned in his hard Algerian experiences, permeated with its sweet spirit all of the story.

See him, old *Don Quixote,* a ridiculous figure in a way and yet a most delightful gentleman filled with generous and high minded sentiments. In spite of the absurdity of his adventures he is always courteous and kindly, the champion of the down-trodden and the protector of the weak. From the name Don Quixote the word "quixotic" has crept into nearly every language in the civilized world and conveys precisely the knight's character. It means a man with impossible, extravagantly romantic and chivalrous notions, who is yet a true champion of the right and a real reformer at heart. Great as the book was, however, nobody guessed in those days that it was to be one of the greatest books in the world, translated into more foreign languages than any other, except the *Bible* and *Pilgrim's Progress*.

Cervantes continued to live for some time after this in squalid poverty, cooped up with his family in the poorest part of Vallodolid. In 1616 he died in Madrid and was buried with no ceremony. No stone or inscription marks his grave. Thirty years later, when Lope de Vega died, grandees bore his coffin, bishops officiated at his funeral and the ceremonies lasted nine days. Ah! when will the world learn to judge the real value of men! Today, Lope de Vega with all his splendor, is quite forgotten, while few names are more highly honored everywhere than that of Miguel de Cervantes.

Don Quixote retold by Judge Parry, illustrated in color by Walter Crane.

CHAMISSO, ALBERT von (French-German, 1781–1838)

Albert von Chamisso was a young French boy of noble family who was obliged to flee from France in the terrible days of the French Revolution. He became a page to the Queen of Prussia and later served his term in the German Army. He wrote very charmingly, both poetry and prose, but in his adopted language, German, not in his native French. The best known of his stories was told to amuse the children of a friend, and has been translated into many foreign languages. It is the *Story of Peter Schlemihl*, the tale of a man who lost his shadow.

CHAPMAN, ARTHUR (American, 1873–)

Arthur Chapman was born in Rockford, Illinois. He was at one time reporter on the Chicago Daily News and later managing editor of the Denver Times. He is the author of two volumes of poetry, chiefly poems of the west.

Important Works: Out Where the West Begins. Cactus Center

CHAUCER, GEOFFREY (English, 1340–1400)

IN days when all the fire of chivalry still burned in knightly breasts, there dwelt at the court of Edward III in England, a young page named Geoffrey Chaucer. Clad in red and black breeches, with a short cloak and elegant shoes, he attended upon his mistress, the wife of Prince Lionel, Edward's son, at many a gay festivity at court. Much he learned there of the ways of gentles, and many a time he sat in some tapestried chamber, amid embroidered lords and ladies, while someone read a graceful poem in French of the style then fashionable at court. Ere long, young Geoffrey himself began to write poems after the manner of the French.

When he was barely nineteen, Geoffrey went off over seas with the King to the wars in France. There he conducted himself right nobly until he was taken prisoner in a disastrous English retreat. For some months he languished in captivity, but he stood so well in favor with the King, that Edward himself at last paid his ransom. Thereafter, behold Geoffrey in the King's own household and risen to be a squire with an annual salary and a gift of a suit of clothes each Christmas-tide. Soon, too, he wedded one of the Queen's demoiselles, a lady named Philippa.

A man of kindly and gentle humor and great courtliness was Chaucer, and as the years passed on, his royal master sent him on more than one important diplomatic mission to foreign parts, now to Genoa, now on a very secret affair to Flanders, and now to France. What a deal of the world Geoffrey Chaucer saw on his travels, and how he was touched with the warm-glowing charm of Italy! Thenceforth, the poems he wrote were no more after the graceful and tender but slight and shallow manner of the French. They were full of the rich life and color of Italy's powerful writers, Dante, Petrarch and Boccaccio.

But Chaucer was not only a courtier, a poet, a soldier, a diplomat. He was also a man of business. For some years he was

Comptroller of Customs at the Port of London and had to be continually at the wharves. His business was to watch the trade in wools, in hides and skins, and with his very own hands to make a record of the same. On the wharves he made acquaintance with stevedores and sea-going men and saw human nature of quite a different sort from that he had known at court. Indeed, whatever task throughout his life Geoffrey's royal masters set him, and he lived in the reigns of three different kings, Edward III, Richard II and Henry IV, he always performed the same with credit, whether it were the carpenter's task of erecting a scaffold at Smithfield whence the King and Queen might view the jousts, or the diplomat's task of arranging a marriage for his King. The height of his success came in 1386 when he sat in Parliament in all his glory as a Knight of the Shire from Kent. Thereafter Chaucer's opponents at court gained the upper hand. He was deprived of most of his offices and obliged, henceforth, to live in comparative poverty.

But now what new life for his poetry! At last he wrote no more after the French or Italian fashion but developed a full, rich English style of his own. Heretofore, French had been the language of the court and English regarded as rude and vulgar, but Chaucer was the first great poet to make the homely English tongue the language of a new and splendid literature. His greatest work was **Canterbury Tales*, a rich and colorful picture of Old

**Chaucer Story Book by Eva March Tappan: Story of the Canterbury Pilgrims by F. J. H. Darton*

England in those stirring Middle Ages. There they wend their way along the white and dusty Kentish road, that company of pilgrims on their horses, journeying to the shrine at Canterbury. From every walk of life they come,—knight, squire, monk and miller, doctor, merchant, meanest churl; and as they journey they tell their precious tales, now one all courtliness of phrase, now the broad and coarser humor of the churl, and, throughout, such vivacity of movement, such tender play of feeling, such rich and merry humor and such delight in nature, in all the "smale foweles" that "maken melodye," the wood-dove and the throstle, in sunshine and soft breezes, in April's fresh, sweet showers. The greatest poet of his period was Geoffrey Chaucer, and when he died he was the first of England's poets to be buried in Westminster Abbey, now sacred to the memory of the greatest of her great.

COLERIDGE, SAMUEL TAYLOR (English, 1772–1824)

There was once a youth who was so starved and hungry after knowledge, that having gained access to a library through the good offices of a friend, he devoured every book in the place, going straight through the racks from one end to the other! He had many odd and original ideas, too, had Samuel Coleridge, and dreamed many a poet's dream. Being dissatisfied with the world as it was, he once planned a Utopia or ideal state, a brotherly community where selfishness should be no more and only goodness reign. This Utopia he hoped to found on the banks of the Susquehanna River in America and his plan only failed for lack of funds. Later, Coleridge went to live in the lovely Lake Country of England, and became a friend of the poet, Wordsworth. His poems are weird and romantic, like *The Rime of the Ancient Mariner.*

CONKLING, GRACE HAZARD (American, contemporary)

Mrs. Conkling is professor of English at Smith College. For some time she lived in Mexico and many of her poems reflect her enjoyment of things Mexican. Her wonderful little daughter, Hilda, has written a volume of most beautiful child verse.

Important Works: Afternoons of April Wilderness Songs
Poems by a Little Girl, by Hilda Conkling

COOKE, EDMUND VANCE (Canadian, 1866–)

Mr. Cooke is a Canadian poet, born in Port Dover, Canada.

COOKE, FLORA J. (American, contemporary)

Miss Cooke is principal of the Francis Parker School, Chicago.

Important Works: Nature Myths for Children.

COOLIDGE, SUSAN (Sarah Chauncey Woolsey) 1848–1894.

Susan Coolidge was born in Cleveland, Ohio, and came of a family distinguished for its scholars, its cultured men and women. Her most popular children's stories are *The Katy Did Series.*

COOPER, GEORGE (American, 1840– ?)

A writer of songs and poems for children's magazines.

COX, PALMER (Canadian, 1840–)

Palmer Cox was born in Granby, Quebec, a Scotch settlement. Here he grew up, his mind filled with such tales as Scottish people tell of their favorite little elves, the Brownies, who do many a kindly deed for good folk in the dead of night. This is how he came as a man, to write his fascinating stories of *The Brownies.*

CRAIK, DINAH MARIA MULOCH (English, 1826–1887)

Miss Muloch thought her father, a clergyman, did not live up to his principles in his treatment of her mother. So in an indignant moment, she took her mother and brothers away from home and supported them by her writing. After she became Mrs. Craik she wrote her children's stories for her own little ones.

Important Works: Adventures of a Brownie. The Little Lame Prince.

CRANDALL, C. H. (American, 1858–)

A reporter, correspondent and editor of *The New York Tribune.*

Important Works: Chords of Life. Wayside Music

CROKER, THOMAS CROFTON (Irish, 1798–1854)

An Irish antiquary and humorist, born in Cork.

Important Works: Fairy Legends of the South of Ireland. Legends of the Lakes

DASENT, SIR GEORGE WEBB (English, 1817–1896)

An English scholar and author who wrote chiefly of the Norse.

Important Works: The Norsemen in Ireland. Story of Burnt Njal. Heroes of Iceland. Vikings of the Baltic.

DICKENS, CHARLES (English, 1812–1870)

IN a dirty, grimy blacking factory in London, amongst the roughest companions, once worked a delicate little fellow named Charles Dickens. He was only nine years old, shabbily dressed and underfed, and day after day he drudged, week in and week out, pasting blue labels on pots of blacking. His mother was a sweet and energetic lady, but his father was of that kindly, easy-going sort who can never support their families, and now he was shut up in the wretched Marshalsea, the squalid prison where men were confined who could not pay their debts. The boy's work was bitterly uncongenial to him. He longed so to go to school and in his secret heart had always dwelt the ambition to be a "learned and distinguished man."

When he was still a small child, Charles had lived in the country. In those days his father owned a few good books which the boy devoured with eagerness. For weeks at a time he was not Charles Dickens at all, but was living in fancy the life of some one of his heroes. Armed with a broken rod from an old pair of boot-trees, he would be Captain Somebody or other of the Royal British Navy. Then he would be beset by savages and purchase his life at the cost of a fearful scrimmage. Every barn in the neighborhood, every stone in the church, every foot of the churchyard had some association in his mind connected with his books. Now he sees one of his heroes climbing the village church steeple; now there stands another with knapsack at his back, stopping to rest by the wicket gate, and over at the village ale-house in the genial firelight, there he sees quite clearly a certain club of worthies from his books holding their evening gossip. Sometimes the little fellow, with his fancies and his secret ambitions, would tramp for miles just to look at an elegant red brick house that stood on Gad's Hill and imagine to himself that it was his and he lived in it.

But now here he was in London, living in wretched squalor, carrying things to sell to the pawn-broker, tying up pots of blacking and visiting his father in the miserable Marshalsea. The contrast of such an existence with the ideals of his fancy served to impress all the more strongly on his mind the odd scenes and queer characters of that poor and dirty London. In spite of his unhappiness he began, too, to see the humorous side of men and things, to draw funny pictures of the barber who came to shave his uncle, and the charwoman who helped his mother.

At length his father got out of prison and Charles was allowed two years of schooling at Mornington. But he was soon forced to go to work again and now had time only for spare moments of study in the British Museum. By the time he was nineteen, however, he had fitted himself to be a reporter and heard and reported the lively discussions in Parliament, sitting up in the gallery.

When he was only twenty-two, Dickens wrote some sketches which were published as *Sketches by Boz*. These became popular at once, and three years later *Pickwick Papers* made him famous. A novelist of the poor, before all else, was Charles Dickens, and how wonderfully rich and varied was his knowledge of all types of men and women from the London streets, knowledge gained in that hard school of the blacking factory. True, he saw men and women in a delicious vein of humor, but he often wrote most seriously, too. He can make you cry as well as laugh and his books always win your sympathy for the poor and the oppressed. Altogether, he made the world more charitable in its judgments and left it a far more tender and gracious place than he found it.

So, at last, Charles Dickens became indeed a "distinquished man," and bought for his own that elegant, red brick house on Gad's Hill, where he lived for the rest of his days.

Important Works: *David Copperfield* *Great Expectations* *Oliver Twist* *Dombey and Son* *Old Curiosity Shop* *Christmas Carol*

DICKINSON, EMILY (American, 1830–1886)

All her life long Emily Dickinson lived in Amherst, Massachusetts, a life most people would have thought intolerably dull, but to Emily herself it was rich and full. She knew intimately all the country round about. To every bud, bird and butterfly she was kin. She wrote poetry, too, startling and original verse, bound by no laws of rhyme or rhythm, but full of vigor and deep convictions. "The mere sense of living is joy enough!" she once said. To her, God was an ever-present friend and death a freer living.

DODGE, MARY MAPES (American, 1838–1905)

Mary Mapes Dodge was the daughter of an eminent writer and scientist whom she often helped in his work. She lived in New York as a child and studied under tutors but never went to school. Only a few years after her marriage she was left a widow with two small boys and she took up writing as a means of support. From reading *Motley's Dutch Republic* she was inspired to write *Hans Brinker*, every chapter of which was submitted for criticism to two Dutchmen who lived near. Once, her own son went into a shop in Amsterdam and asked for a good book to read. The shop-keeper handed him *Hans Brinker*. In 1873 Mrs. Dodge became the first editor of *St. Nicholas* and it was she who made it a leading magazine.

DRAKE, JOSEPH RODMAN (American, 1795–1820)

An American poet, of the same family as Admiral Drake.

EATON, WALTER PRICHARD (American, 1878–)

A dramatic critic and writer of delightful nature essays. He once lived in New York, but on a vacation trip he was entranced by a beautiful garden in Stockbridge, Mass. and went back to the City only long enough to pack up his possessions.

Important Works: Boy Scouts in Glacier Park On the Edge of the Wilderness

EELS, ELSIE SPICER (American, contemporary)

Mrs. Eels is a specialist in Hispanic folk lore. She spent three years in Brazil where her husband was superintendent of the schools established by the Presbyterian Board of Missions.

Important Works: Tales of Enchantment from Spain Fairy Tales from Brazil

ELIOT, GEORGE (Mary Ann Evans) English, 1819–1880

ON a bright, frosty morning, in old England's picturesque stage-coach days, a little girl and her brother stood before the gate of Griff House, just at the bend of the highroad, waiting eagerly for His Majesty's mail coach to go dashing by. And now they hear the far-off, ringing beat of the horses' hoofs on the ground. Ah! there the great coach comes flashing into view with its four gallant greys at full speed—coachman and guard aloft in scarlet, outside passengers muffled in furs, and baskets and bulky packages dangling merrily at the rear.

That coach was the chief connecting link between Griff and the outside world, and little Mary Ann Evans and her brother, Isaac, watched for it every day. For Griff was a country place in the Midland section of England and remote enough from the world it seemed in those days of no railways, no penny post, and no telegraph. A charming, red brick, ivy-covered house it was, on the Arbury estate which Mary Ann's father managed for its owner. Here, day in and day out, the little brother and sister played. Mary Ann was always at her brother's heels, doing whatever he did, and nothing was missing at Griff House to make them happy. There was a delightful, old-fashioned garden, a pond and a canal to fish in. There were farm offices close to the house, a long cow-shed and a broad shouldered barn, where butter and cheese were made by their energetic mother.

An affectionate and impulsive but proud little Maggie Tulliver was Mary Ann, and sensitive to the highest degree, moved easily to either smiles or tears. Moreover, she was always troubled by jealousy in her affections. All her life long she wanted to be all in all to somebody and have somebody all in all to her. How then could she fail but be often most unhappy? In her childhood, the somebody whom she loved so jealously was Isaac, her brother. She had an older sister, Christiana, or "Chrissy," who was always as neat and tidy as Mary Ann was frowsy-haired and wild. But

Chrissy, because of her neatness, was a great favorite with her three worthy aunts, Mrs. Evans' sisters, who were doubtless very like Maggie Tulliver's aunts, the highly superior Dodsons, and she used to spend a great deal of time with them, so that the younger boy and girl were left much alone together. But, alas! Mary Ann's jealous affection for Isaac suffered tortures when they were separated, he to go to boys' school, and she to a girls'. How she looked forward then to the coming of the holidays and how anxious she was when he came home to know all that he had been doing and learning since they parted. And when she was seven years old and Isaac was given a pony, to which he grew so attached that he cared less and less to play with her, Mary Ann was nearly broken-hearted.

In those days, if one had looked into the Griff dining room on a Saturday night after tea, he would have seen a pretty sight. There in the deep, leather-covered armchair at the right of the ruddy fire-place sits the father, powerful and middle-aged, with strongly-marked features. Between his knees crouches Mary Ann, and he is explaining to her a pretty book of pictures. Her features are strong like her father's, and her rebellious hair is all in her eyes, much to the sorrow of her mother who sits busily knitting on the opposite side of the fire. Near the mother, all prim and tidy, is the older sister with her work, and between the two groups is the boy, who keeps assuring himself by perpetual search that none of his favorite means of amusement is escaping from his pockets!

Mr. Evans was already very proud of the astonishing and growing intellect of his little girl. Now, when she came home for the holidays, she and Isaac would devise and act out charades before their aunts and the Griff household, and these were so cleverly done that even the aunts had to admit that their niece of the rebellious hair was a person of real ability.

From a very early age Mary Ann was accustomed to accompany her father on his drives through the neighborhood. Standing between his knees as he drove leisurely along, she drank in eager impressions of the country and its people. In the Warwickshire of those days they passed rapidly from one phase of English life to another. Now they drove through the countryside with green fields and hedge-rows stretching away as far as the eye could see, and all the people they met were farmers and countryfolk; now they passed a fine old park which shut in some noble mansion house and allowed just a glimpse of its treasure to shine here and there through the trees. Grey steeples there were, too, pricking the sky, and green and shady churchyards. Then, in another moment they would come upon barren land all blackened with coal-pits, and look down suddenly over a village dingy and dirty with coal dust. Soon they would clatter along on the pavement of a manufacturing town. Powerful men they saw here, grimy with

coal dust and walking queerly with knees bent outward from long squatting in the mines. These men were going home to throw themselves down in their blackened flannels and sleep through the daylight. In the evening they would rise and spend a good share of their wages at the ale-houses with their fellows. Everywhere were poor cottages and small, dirty children, and over all the busy noise of the loom. From windows and doorways peered the pale, eager faces of the handloom weavers, both men and women, haggard with sitting up late at night to finish their toilsome labors. These people made a deep impression on Mary Ann. They had no right whatever to vote, and had long been ground down by the tyranny of their masters. Such towns were often the scene of trades-union meetings and riots, and once, when Mary Ann was thirteen years old, she saw one of these riots in the town of Nuneaton. It was in the year 1832, when the King had been forced, after determined opposition, to let the Reform Bill pass, and for the very first time, the poorer people had been given the right to vote for members of Parliament. So eager were they to elect their own candidate and keep out the representative of the wealthier classes, that they formed in a mob threatening and attacking those who wished to vote for their opponents. The magistrate had to call out the Scots Greys to quell the riot, but on the arrival of the soldiers the tumult increased until it assumed alarming proportions. The magistrates themselves were attacked and injured in the very discharge of their duties. Several officers of the Scots Greys were wounded and two or three men, who were attempting to reach the polls, were dragged from the protecting files of soldiers, cruelly beaten and stripped naked. This unhappy outburst of hatred, caused by so many years of cppression, was never forgotten by Mary Ann.

An old fashioned child she was, living in a world of her own imaginations, impressionable to her finger tips, thinking deeply already, and often at odds with the hard and fast accepted beliefs of her time. She was full, too, of an eager love for all that was beautiful and longed in her inmost heart to achieve something great, though she often blackly despaired of ever doing anything.

When Mary Ann was sixteen years old her mother died, and soon after this her brother and sister married, so that she became, henceforth, housekeeper and sole companion to her dearly beloved father. As long as he lived she spent the greater part of her time with him in their remote country home. But when he died, she found her way, through the help of friends, out into the greater world. For years, now, she wrote and wrote, translations and articles, translations and articles, but it was not until she was a woman of middle age that she found the work which really made her famous. It was suggested to her then that she write a novel, and what should she write about but that old Midland English life which she knew so well and with which she had sympathized so deeply? All at once she found that she could write of men and women so truly and sympathetically that here lay her real life work. Under the name of George Eliot she published a number of novels.

George Eliot was the first English novelist to see in life simply human character developing, and to find all the stirring comedy and tragedy of her books, not in outward events, but in the hearts and souls of men, their inward victories and defeats. And so the little girl of Griff House became England's greatest woman novelist.

Important Works: Silas Marner Romola The Mill on the Floss

EMERSON, RALPH WALDO (American, 1803–1882)

One of America's greatest essayists, philosophers, and poets, who inspired men to a better faith in themselves and to less reliance for happiness or success upon outward things.

See also Alcott, Louisa. Page 16

EWING, JULIANA HORATIA (English, 1841–1885)

Mrs. Ewing was an English writer of simple, unaffected children's stories which have great charm and interest.

Important Works: Jackanapes Lob-lie-by-the-fire Jan of the Windmill

FABRE, JEAN HENRI* (French, 1823–1915)

THERE goes little Henri, barefooted, bareheaded, with his soiled frieze smock flapping against his heels. He is coming home from the tiny hamlet of Malaval where he has been living with his grandam and his grandad, horny-handed folk who till the soil. A solitary place it was, the cottage at Malaval, standing so lone amidst the broom and heather, with no neighbor for miles around. Sometimes thieving wolves came sneaking by, and the country round about was a wild solitude, mossy fens and quagmires oozing with iridescent pools. But the house itself was a cozy place, its barnyard swarming with lambs and geese and pigs, its big room glowing with lurid light from the fire which brings into bright relief the eager faces of children, crowding around the table. Each child has a spoon and a wooden bowl before him, and there at one end of the table, his unclipped hair like a shaggy mane, sits Grandad, cutting with vigorous stroke an enormous rye loaf the size of a cart-wheel. Armed with a long metal ladle, Grandma is dipping the supper from a capacious pot that bubbles lustily over the flames. Um! how good it smells, the savor of bacon and turnips! After supper, Grandma takes up her distaff and spindle in the corner by the hearth and tells the children stories as they squat in the fire-light before her, stories of dragons and serpents and wolves.

Little Henri loves those stories, but he loves something else better still, for which the others laugh at him. He finds a whole fairy world for himself by watching the queer insects that abound in that countryside. Little six-year-old monkey! He will stand in ecstasy before the splendor of the gardener beetle's wing-cases, or the wings of a butterfly. All the dazzling beauty of their shimmering color is as magic unto him. Once he heard a little singing, faint and soft among the bushes at night-fall. What was it? A little

**Told chiefly from the autobiographical chapters in* The Life of the Fly.

bird? He must discover. True, he dares not venture too far away. There are wolves about, you know. Just there it is, the sound, behind that clump of broom. The boy puts out his hand. In vain! At the faintest little noise the brushwood jingle ceases. At last! Whoosh! A grab of the hand and he holds the singer fast. It is not a bird; it is a kind of grasshopper, and the boy knows now from his own observation that the grasshopper sings.

Ah, well-a-day! Now he is going back to the town of St. Léons in southern France where he was born. His father has sent for him to go to school. The schoolmaster of St. Léons is Henri's godfather, and what a man he is! He is not only schoolmaster; he is village barber as well and shaves all the notables, the mayor and parish priest. He is the bell-ringer who must interrupt his lessons to ring a merry peal for a wedding or a christening. He is choirmaster and fills the church with his mighty voice at vespers. He is care-taker of the village clock and climbs every day to the top of the steeple where he opens a huge cage of rafters and performs some miraculous windings amidst a maze of wheels and springs. He is manager of the property of an absentee landlord, directs the getting in of the hay, the walnuts, the apples and oats; he takes care of an old vacant castle with four great towers which are now

but so many houses for pigeons. Such time as he has left from these duties he gives to his teaching! And the room where little Henri goes to school! It is at once a school, a kitchen, a bedroom, a dining room, a chicken house and a piggery! There is a ladder leading up out of it to the loft above, whence the schoolmaster sometimes brings down hay for his ass, or a basket of potatoes for the house-wife. That loft is the only other room in the house. The school room has a monumental fire-place, adorned with enormous bellows and a shovel so huge that it takes two hands to lift it. On either side of the hearth are recesses in the wall. These recesses are beds, and each has two sliding planks that serve as doors and shut in the sleeper at night, so he may lie cozy and snug while the North-wind howls without. Over in the sunny nook by the window stands the master's desk, and opposite, in a wall-niche, gleam a copper water-pail and rows of shining pewter dishes. Well nigh every spot on the wall that is touched by the light is adorned with a gay-colored half-penny picture. There is the lovely Genevieve of Brabant with her roe, and the fierce villain, Golo, hiding, sword in hand, darkly in the bushes. There is the Wandering Jew with hobnailed boots and a stout stick, his long, white beard falling, like an avalanche of snow, over his apron to his knees. What a source of constant delight to Henri are these pictures! How they hold his eye with their color—great patches of red, blue and green!

On three-legged stools before the hearth sit the little scholars, and there before them, in an enormous cauldron over the flames, hangs the pigs' food, simmering and giving off jets of steam with a puff-puff-puffing sound. Sometimes the boys take care to leave the school room door open. Then the little porkers, attracted by the smell of the food, come running in. They go trotting up to Henri, grunting and curling their little tails, questioning with their sharp little eyes, and poking their cold, pink snouts into his hand in search of a chestnut or scrap of bread. The master flicks his handkerchief—snick! Off go the little pigs! All to no use! A moment later, behold, in the doorway, old Madame Hen with her velvet-coated brood! The boys crumble pieces of bread and vie with each other to call the little chicks to them. Ah! their backs are so downy and soft to tickle with your fingers!

It was not much little Henri could learn in such a school. No! he held a book up in front of his face but he never even learned his letters! One day his father brings him home a gaily-colored print, divided into squares, in each of which an animal teaches the alphabet by means of his name. A is for Ass, and so on! Little Henri is overjoyed. Those speaking pictures bring him among his friends. Animals forever! The beasts have taught him his letters!

But now where shall he keep his precious print? He has a little sanctum that he has appropriated to himself in their humble home. It is a window in a cozy recess like the schoolmaster's. From there he can overlook the whole village as it straggles along the hillside. Way down in the hollow is the church with its three steeples and its clock. A little higher up lies the village square where a fountain falls from basin to basin beneath a high-arched roof. Sprinkled over the slopes above, lie little houses with garden patches rising in terraces banked up by tottering walls. Between, are steep lanes cut out of the solid rock, lanes so steep that even the sure-footed mules, with their loads of branches, hesitate to enter them. High above all, standing out against the sky, a few wind-battered oaks bristle on the ridges. Those trees are Henri's friends and he loves them dearly. In stormy weather they bow their heads and turn their backs to the wind. They bend and toss about as though to uproot themselves and take to flight. How often has Henri watched them writhing like madmen when the North-wind's besom raises the snow-dust; and then tomorrow they stand motionless, still and upright, against a fair blue sky. What are they doing up there, those desolate trees? He is gladdened by their calmness and distressed by their terrified gestures. They are his friends. In the morning the sun rises behind their transparent screen and ascends in its glory. Where does it come from? To the boy, those trees seem the boundary of the world. In this cozy little sanctum, with such an outlook, Henri keeps all his treasures. It is not too many treasures that he is allowed to keep.

Once he was sent up the hillside by the path that climbed behind the chateau to the pond. He was to lead their twenty-four downy ducklings to the water. What a delight that pond was to him. On the warm mud of its edge the Frog's baby, the little Tadpole, basks and frisks in its black legions. At the bottom are beautiful shells and little worms carrying tufts and feathers. Above, the reeds and water are swarming with busy life. It is a whole immense world for Henri to observe. What are all those little creatures about? What are they doing? What are their names? While the ducklings rummage delightedly, head-downward and stern-upward in the water, Henri looks carefully about. There are some soot-colored knots like strands of old yarn in the mud. He lifts one up. It slips sticky and slack through his fingers, but look! a few of the knots have burst, and out comes a black globule the size of a pinhead, followed by a flat tail. He recognizes, on a small scale, the Frog's baby, the Tadpole, and has found out that these are her eggs. Enough! he disturbs the knots of yarn no more.

When he goes home that night his pockets are bulging with treasures. He has found stones that glitter like diamonds, and something like gold dust amidst the sand. On the alder trees he has found that beautiful beetle, the sacred scarab. It is of an unutterable blue, a living jewel that pales the azure of the sky. He puts the glorious one in an empty snail shell which he plugs up with a leaf. He will take it home to observe it at leisure. But when he reaches the cottage and mother and father see his pockets like to be torn to pieces by their burden his father cries:

"You rascal! I send you to mind the ducks and you amuse yourself by picking up stones. Make haste, throw them away!"

Broken-hearted, he obeys. Diamonds, gold-dust, petrified ram's-horn, heavenly beetle, all are flung on the ash-heap!

The brook that runs through the village is also a source of constant delight to Henri,—dear little brook, so tranquil, cool and clear. Half-way up the hillside a miller has dammed it to make a reservoir for his mill-wheel. The reservoir is shut off from the road by a melancholy wall, all darkly bearded with ferns, but one day little Henri hoists himself up on a playfellow's shoulders and peers over. Bottomless, stagnant water he sees, covered with slimy, green scum, and in the gaps of that carpet, there lazily swims a black and yellow reptile! Ha! the very serpent or dragon of his grandmother's fireside tales it seems. Henri loses no time. He slips down again in a hurry. Years later he knows he had seen a salamander.

Below the reservoir, alders and ash bend forward on either side of the brook, a lofty arch of living green. At the foot of the trees the great twisted roots form watery caverns prolonged into gloomy corridors. On the threshold of these fastnesses shimmers only a glint of sunshine that sifts down through the leaves overhead. This is the haunt of the red-necktied minnow. Come along very gently. Lie flat on the ground and look. What pretty little fish they are with their scarlet throats. See them there clustering side by side and rinsing their mouths incessantly. No movement save the slightest quiver of their tails and the fin on their backs to keep them still in running water. On a sudden a leaf drops down from the tree. Whoosh! the whole troop disappears!

On the other side of the brook is a cluster of beeches with smooth straight trunks like pillars. In the shade of those majestic branches sit chattering crows. The ground below is padded with moss, and at Henri's first step on that downy carpet his eye is caught by what?—it must be an egg dropped there by some

vagrant hen. No! It is that curious thing, a mushroom, not yet full spread. It is the first he has ever picked and he turns it about in his fingers inquiring into its structure. Soon he finds another differing in size and shape and color. Ah! what a great treat it is! This one is bell-shaped, that one is like a cup; others are drawn out into spindles, hollowed into funnels or rounded like hemispheres. He comes upon one that is broken and weeping milky tears. He steps upon another and it all turns blue in an instant. Ah! but here is one shaped like a pear with a little hole at the top like a sort of chimney. He prods the under side with his fingers. A whiff of smoke shoots up from the chimney! Amusing! How amusing! Henri has found a puff ball.

Plants and insects and animals,—on every side, what things, of interest in the world. Among the golden buttercups of the meadows, the blue campanulas of the hills, the pink heather of the mountains, the fragrant bracken of the woods, what treasures Henri finds! And the birds! Once he was climbing the hill with an apple for his lunch, to visit his friends, the trees, and explore the edge of the world. But what is this at his feet? A lovely bird has flown from its hiding place under the eaves of a stone. Bless us! here is a nest made of hair and fine straw, and in it six eggs laid so prettily side by side. Those eggs are a magnificent blue, as though steeped in the blue of the sky. Overpowered with happiness, Henri lies down on the grass and stares, while the mother, with a little clap of her gullet—Tack! Tack! flits anxiously near by. It is the first nest which Henri has ever found, the first of the joys which the birds are to bring him.

But when Henri is twelve years old his father moves away from the country and goes to the town to keep a cafe. Now

Henri may go to school where he can really learn. His father, however, is never truly successful. He is always poor. Bad days come again when Henri must leave his lessons and earn his bread as best he may, now selling lemons under the arcades of the market at the fair of Beaucaire, or before the barracks of the Pré, another day enlisting in a gang of day-laborers to work on the road. Gloomy days those were, lonely and despairing, but in spite of all, the boy's love of nature and his passion for learning upheld him. Often, too, some creature kept him company, some insect never seen before. Today he is hungry, but he finds for the first time the pine-chafer, that superb beetle whose black or chestnut coat is sprinkled with specks of white velvet, and which squeaks when you capture him, with a slight complaining sound. Enough! Henri's hunger is forgotten.

When he is nineteen, Henri takes a competitive examination and enters the normal school of Carpentras. He finishes the very simple schooling there, and then, little as he knows, he begins to teach others. What a teacher he is, studying right along with his pupils and learning through teaching them, puzzling out for himself, with passionate devotion, every branch of science, and teaching as he goes. Now he holds his chemistry class with rudest, home-made instruments, in the dusky, vaulted nave of an old, abandoned, Gothic church, which has once seemed to him like some wizard's den, with its rusty, old weather-cock creaking atop its steeple, the great bats flitting among the gargoyles and the owls hooting on the roof. Now he takes his pupils out among the fields to study nature "at the ineffable festival of the awakening of life in the Spring."

His pupils love him dearly, but alas! education is still held in little esteem in France.

DONN P. CRANE

The salary paid Professor Fabre is but a paltry pittance. He is married, too, and has a family to keep. How can he make both ends meet? Only by teaching, teaching, teaching, and that leaves him so little time to study his precious insects. He is peculiar, too, is Professor Fabre, and finds little favor with his fellow teachers. In the simplicity of his heart he cares nothing for worldly honors, for the forms and ceremonies of the world. He cares only to study and to learn. He does not like to wear the long, slick, black coat and high silk hat befitting a Professor. Fie! There goes Professor Fabre in a little slouch hat! It is unseemly! He must be reprimanded! He must wear a "topper" like his fellows! And so it goes. For thirty years of patient struggle, so it goes. But now, at last, he has acquired a modest income from his writings. He can leave off teaching and buy a little house at Sérignan. Glory be! he can doff his professor's coat and don the peasant's blouse again! He can plant a flower in his old silk hat, and when it has served its time as a flowerpot he can kick it into bits! He is free for his studies!

A pink house with green shutters, half hidden among trees, was the hermitage at Sérignan, and its garden a riot of verdure, the sweet air full of insects humming and heavy with perfume. Here those little creatures each told the student its secret and its history. How he loved them all, how tenderly he wrote of them, how accurately he observed them. Other scientists dissected insects and sought the secret of their life from death; Fabre observed his alive and sought the secret of their life from the marvelous instinct that directed all their ways. With reverence and awe he stood before the unerring Power that guides the wild bee and the wasp, though they may be carried miles away from home, back over vast and unknown spaces, surely to their nests. In instinct he saw the lofty evidence of God. How wonderfully those little creatures built their nests, how certain was the power that guided them, how surely each fulfilled his given task. True, the ugliness he saw in that little world troubled his tender spirit,—the cannibalism, the brutality of manners, the murders and assassinations. Here was something to wish done away. But far above all else, he marveled at the wonderful intelligence that directed there, and throughout nature he adored the great Eternal Power whose imprint is everywhere.

Studying in his sunny garden, Fabre not only loved insects himself, but he also taught others to love them. He was the first to cast away in his writings the long words and dry scientific phrases which other scientists used and which seemed to him like some barbarous Iroquois tongue. He wrote as the poet writes. For him the cricket was not some creature with a long Latin name, but "the brown violinist of the clods," and that voracious diving beetle that feeds on all the other insects of the water, was not the Dytiscus only, but the "pirate of the ponds." He tells us how at break of day "the bee pops her head out of her attic window to see what the weather is" and how "the timid spider of the thickets suspends by ethereal cables the branching whorls of his snare which the tears of the night have turned into chaplets of jewels." What fairy tale could equal to him the wonder of the butterfly bursting from the cocoon, or the marvelous unfolding of the locust's iridescent wings? He had his flesh-eating ogres too, his pirates and assassins, his modest and industrious little workers with their thousand curious callings, and his pigmy princes clad in gold and purple, dazzling with embroidery, adorned with lofty plumes, displaying their diamonds, their topazes and sapphires, gleaming with fire or shining like mirrors, magnificant of mien. To him, the best fairy book ever written could be read by simply upturning a stone. And so little Henri discovered the Fairyland of Science and revealed it to the world.

Important Works: The Story Book of Science   Life of the Spider   Life of the Fly

FAULKNER, GEORGENE (American contemporary, 1873–)

"The Story Lady" is one of Chicago's favorite story tellers. Dressed in costume, she often tells stories of foreign lands.

Important Works: Italian Story Book   Old Russian Tales

FIELD, EUGENE (American, 1850–1895)

THE "feller" who knew so much about "Seein' Things at Night" and all his life long had the heart of a boy, was born in St. Louis, but his mother died when he was seven years old and he was brought up by a cousin in Amherst, Massachusetts. His grandmother had high hopes of turning him out a minister and used to offer him ninepence to write her a sermon. O, what ridiculous sermons he wrote! But the boy, who always had a merry twinkle in his eye, did not grow up to be a preacher. He became a newspaper man and the beloved poet of childhood. For twelve years he worked on the Chicago *Daily News* but his heart was most at one with the children who played on the vacant lots near his home. And what a man he was for a joke! If he felt that an increase of salary was his due, could he go and ask for it in the ordinary way? No, not he! He must appear in the office of his Chief dressed in rags, with four of his children likewise in rags. They all make pleading gestures, fall on their knees and pretend to weep, while he cries beseechingly, "Please, Mr. Stone, can't you see your way to raise my salary?"

Tenderness, beauty, fun, love of fairies, witches and childhood,—all these he preserved in the midst of Chicago's work-a-day world.

Important Works: Poems of Childhood. Lullaby Land. With Trumpet and Drum.

FRANCE, ANATOLE (Anatole Thibaut) French, 1844–

The light and air of Paris were the native atmosphere of little Anatole Thibaut. As a child he watched the dairy girls carrying milk and the coal-heavers, coal, into all the houses of the Latin Quarter. He lived among the riverside streets and quays of the Seine, where his father was a poor book-seller, and his dearest friends were the wise old books. How he loved the river, too, "which by day mirrored the sky and bore boats on its breast, by night decked itself with jewels and sparkling flowers." He grew up the most French of Frenchmen and, when he began to write, he boldly took the name France in place of Thibaut.

Important Works: Girls and Boys. Our Children (Illustrated by Boutet de Monvel)

FREEMAN, MARY E. WILKINS (American, 1862–)

A Massachusetts woman, who portrays the quaint, homely life of New England. For years the secretary to Oliver Wendell Holmes.

Jerome, A Poor Man *In Colonial Times* *Young Lucretia*

GALSWORTHY, JOHN (English, 1867–)

AN earnest, stick-to-it-ive boy was John Galsworthy, not surprisingly brilliant, but sure and steady. He comes of an old Saxon family from Devonshire and was born at Combe in Surrey. At Harrow and Oxford he received the typical education of an English gentleman, after which he was off for several years of travel in foreign lands—to Russia, Canada, Australia, New Zealand, South Africa and the far-off Fiji Islands. On an old-fashioned sailing ship off Australia he met the novelist, Joseph Conrad, then still a sailor, and the two became fast friends.

When Galsworthy returned to England he began to write,—novels, poems, plays. *Strife*, a gripping play presenting the strife between Capital and Labor, first really showed that he could so influence men as to bring about reform. *Justice*, written to reveal the hideous suffering caused by the cold wheels of English law, as it ground over criminals like some mechanical thing with neither sympathy nor intelligence, so moved Secretary Churchill that he set about reforms which have changed the English prison system.

GARLAND, HAMLIN (American, 1860–)

Hamlin Garland was a farm boy of the Middle West, born in Wisconsin and educated in Iowa. Later he took up a claim in Dakota, but he soon made off to Boston and began writing stories.

Boy Life on the Prairie *The Long Trail (Klondike)*

GAUTIER, JUDITH (French, 1850–)

A French writer of plays, poems and historical novels, daughter of Theophile Gautier, the famous novelist, and wife of Pierre Loti, another noted writer. She is a student of Oriental life and language and knows both Chinese and Japanese well.

The Memoirs of a White Elephant

*GOLDSMITH OLIVER (Irish, 1728–1774)

POOR little Doctor Goldsmith, with his kindly eyes, his squat little figure, his awkward, ungainly legs, his pale, pock-marked face and that absurd love of fine clothes! How everybody laughed at him, though sometimes with tears, and how they all loved him. Now, if his fortunes were poor, his coat was bought second hand, a tarnished green and gold with an ugly patch on the breast, but he strutted along just as proudly and carefully hid the patch by holding his hat well over it; now, when his fortunes were fine, he blossomed out in peach-color, claret, sky-blue! And yet, in spite of his vanity and a thousand other weaknesses, what a great, generous, loving heart! Who could do other than love him?

He had always a crowd of children at his heels, had little Doctor Goldsmith. His favorite enjoyment was to romp with them, the merriest and noisiest of all. Sometimes he played them a tune on his flute, sang them an Irish song, or told them stories of Irish fairies. Again, he led them at blindman's-buff, or a game of hunt-the-slipper. And if the children were very small, he would turn the hind part of his wig before and play scores of tricks to amuse them.

Once he was drinking coffee with a friend and took the friend's little five-year old son up tenderly on his knee. Moved by some perverse instinct, what did the tiny George Coleman do, but rap him a spiteful slap on the face that left a tingling red mark. The father indignantly took his small son and locked him up in another room to suffer for his crime by solitary imprisonment in the dark. But soon, very soon, there was some one come to the little fellow's rescue, some one holding a candle and smiling so tenderly. It was Dr. Goldsmith himself. Georgie sulked and sobbed at first, but Goldsmith fondled and soothed him until he began to brighten. Then the little Doctor placed three hats on the carpet with a shilling under each. "Hey, presto, cockolorum!" he cried. And lo! when he lifted the hats, all three of the shillings were found in a heap

**Read The Jessamy Bride by F. F. Moore, a story of Goldsmith and his time.*

under one! Such wizardry! George Coleman's heart was won!

It was way back in the lonely little hamlet of Pallas, in Ireland, that Oliver Goldsmith was born, in a little old house that the peasant folk said stood on haunted ground, where "the good folk," the fairies, held their nightly revels. But when little Noll was still very young, his father moved to a better home on the outskirts of Lissoy. This home was part parsonage and part farm for Father Goldsmith was a country curate, large of heart and small of means, and as guileless and ignorant of the world as the dear old Vicar of Wakefield. Lissoy was a charming village, too, very like "Sweet Auburn, loveliest village of the plain," with its sheltered little white cottages and cultivated farms.

At the age of six little Noll was sent to the village schoolmaster, Thomas Byrne, and what a man he was! He had served in the Spanish wars, and now, when he should have been teaching the village urchins their sums, he held them spellbound with tales of his vagabond wanderings abroad, adventures of which he, himself, was usually the hero. To this he added tales of fairies, ghosts and banshees, pirates, robbers, smugglers. So, little Noll imbibed in his youth far more of romance than of learning. When he grew older he was sent to a higher school at Edgeworthstown, some twenty miles from Lissoy, and on his last journey home from there, a mere stripling of sixteen, he met with a most absurd adventure.

Little used to money was Oliver Goldsmith, and now a friend had given him a whole round golden guinea to cover his traveling expenses. Noll's head was quite turned by his riches! Off he started on horseback over a road so rough as to be impassable to coaches, determined to play the man and spend his treasure in lavish fashion. For the night he halted at Ardagh, and, intending to ask the whereabouts of the inn, he accosted the very first person he met, demanding with swaggering importance to know where was "the best house in the village." Now it chanced that the man whom he thus encountered was a famous wag and,

amused by the stripling's importance, he directed him literally to "the best house in the village," the family mansion of one, Mr. Featherstone, a gentleman of great fortune. With all the airs in the world, up rides young Noll to the house which he thinks is an inn and orders his horse to be led away to the stable! He then walks into the parlor, seats himself by the fire and curtly demands to know what he can have for supper! The owner of the place, seeing the lad's whimsical mistake, and learning, by chance, that he was the son of an old friend, determined to carry out the joke. So young Goldsmith was fooled to the top of his bent and permitted to have full sway all the evening. Usually Noll was shy and diffident of manner, but thinking himself now among inferiors, he grew very free and easy, showing off and making out that he was a most experienced traveller. When supper was served he condescendingly insisted that the landlord, his wife and daughter should sit at the table and partake of the meal with him, and when he went to bed, as a last flourish of manliness, he gave special orders that a hot cake should be ready for his breakfast. Imagine his dismay next day when he learned he had swaggered thus in the house of a private gentleman! Years later he turned this ludicrous blunder into the play "*She Stoops to Conquer or The Mistakes of a Night*," which set all London laughing.

But Goldsmith's school life, henceforth, was far from happy. He was ugly, awkward and poor, and, moreover, little given to learning. In Trinity College, Dublin, he had to earn his way by holding the position of a servant, and tutors and boys seemed in league together to jeer at and torment him. He was extremely sensitive, too, because, of his ugliness and he added to his misery by seeking riotous friends instead of trying to shine as a student.

Time and again he failed, failed, failed. He was to enter the ministry, but he appeared before the Bishop to seek his appointment in such loud scarlet breeches that the Bishop was scandalized and refused him. He failed at the law; he failed as a student of medicine. So at last he took his flute and off he went alone for a walking tour through Flanders, France and Switzerland. As he journeyed he played on his flute and his tunes set the peasantry dancing and won for him everywhere his supper and a bed.

After wandering through Italy, likewise, he returned to England with no friends and no calling. At length he took a garret in a dark, miserable, little back court that could only be reached by a steep flight of narrow flagstone stairs called Breakneck Steps. Here washings hung out all day and frowsy women quarreled over the washtubs, but for the first time in his life Goldsmith set earnestly to work. He began to write, to drudge at writing, doing whatever the booksellers ordered. Now these were the days when hustling little John Newbery kept his far-famed shop in St. Paul's Churchyard, where the first real children's books were displayed, bound in gilt paper and adorned with queer, old, hideous wood-cuts. Goldsmith did a great deal of work for Newbery, probably editing the first real *Mother Goose* and writing the tale of *Goody Two Shoes*.

But even in such dark days Goldsmith was never bitter. He was always inviting his landlady or some poor child into his rooms to cheer them with a cake or sweetmeat and to play for them on his flute. Moreover, all his life long he believed with childlike simplicity anything that was told him, and many a tale of woe, either true or untrue, wrung from him his last penny. Sometimes, too, with that curious unworldliness that kept him from ever truly understanding money, he gave away things he did not possess. Once his landlady came to him with a sorry tale of her husband cast into the debtor's prison for desperate need of money. Moved to the heart, Goldsmith sold a new suit of clothes which he had not paid for in order to give her the money. He was then called a knave and a sharper by those who had sold him the suit, and nearly went to the debtor's prison himself trying to pay for what he no longer possessed.

Slowly, slowly, however, his writings began to be noticed. Ah! Now he commenced to make worthy friends. At length the great Dr. Samuel Johnson himself, the most famous literary light of the day, became his friend. In 1764 he was one of a group of most remarkable men who formed a club that met regularly, henceforth, at the Turk's Head Tavern. There was the big, burly, important Doctor Johnson, always followed by his humble little satellite, James Boswell, whom he was continually snubbing and who delighted in being snubbed by the great Dr. Johnson. There was Edmund Burke, the brilliant Irish orator, to be known in the days of the American Revolution for his eloquent speech in Parliament on *Conciliation With the Colonies*, and there was the famous portrait painter, Sir Joshua Reynolds. The actor, David Garrick, was likewise a friend of the group. All these great men loved "Goldy," though they often made merciless fun of him.

One day word came to Dr. Johnson that Goldsmith was in great distress and besought him to come to his lodgings at once. Off went Dr. Johnson to find that the landlady at the place where Goldsmith now lived had had him arrested for not paying his rent and a sheriff's officer had him in custody. Goldsmith told Johnson, however, that he had the manuscript of a novel ready for print, but could not go out to sell it because of the officer. Johnson glanced hastily over the manuscript, saw that it had merit, and went out and sold it for sixty pounds ($300). That manuscript was the famous story, *The Vicar of Wakefield*.

Soon after this, Goldsmith's poem, *The Traveller*, appeared, and it was at once pronounced so fine that his friends at the Turk's Head could scarcely believe he had written it. Now, at last, Goldsmith began to prosper and to earn a great deal of money. But alas! funny little man that he was, he would still continue to make such ridiculous blunders. The Duke of Northumberland once sent for him to congratulate him on *The Traveller*. Dressed in his best, Goldsmith sallied forth to Northumberland House, preparing on the way a lot of studied compliments to recite to his noble patron. After he had waited some time in Northumberland House a very grand personage appeared, most elegantly dressed. Taking him for the Duke, "Goldy" delivered unto him all the fine compliments he had prepared. To his great astonishment the man informed him that he was only a servant, and his master would presently appear! As the Duke came in just then, he found Goldsmith so confused that, far from repeating his compliments, he could scarcely stutter a word.

During his latter days Goldsmith became famous and had such delightful friends as the Hornecks, a widow and two lovely daughters, one of whom, Miss Mary, he called affectionately, the Jessamy bride. But in spite of his fame, he never learned how to manage money, and throughout his life he remained the same simple, kind-hearted gentleman whose friends, though they smiled at his blunders, always loved him so dearly.

Vicar of Wakefield   She Stoops to Conquer   The Deserted Village   The Traveller

GRAHAME, KENNETH (Scottish, 1858–   )

A Scottish author, educated in England. Best known for his *Golden Age* and *Dream Days*, stories reminiscent of childhood, and for *The Wind in the Willows*, a charming nature fantasy.

GREENAWAY, KATE (English, 1846–1901)

ROSES and posies and quaint little children in old-fashioned gardens,—what magic in Kate Greenaway's name! Her lovely pictures of children, so dainty and full of grace, seem to breathe forth the very fragrance of prim little, trim little gardens.

A happy little mite was the tiny Kate Greenaway, a London child sent into the country to be nursed by an old family servant. Sometimes she ventured out with her "Nanan" into the grain fields where the wheat towered high above her head. What enchanted vistas opened before her, stretching away forever and ever,—avenues of golden grain made brilliant with scarlet pimpernels, blue and white veronica and gorgeous crimson poppies. But oh! When she could visit her far-off Flowerbank it was more exciting still. There were queer old stiles to be climbed and delightfully terrifying foot-planks to be crossed over such a deep, dark, mysterious stream. Then, away through a shady wood to the mill. In the woods grew the large, blue cranesbill, the purple vetch and wild morning-glory, and up in the trees the wood-pigeons cooed. Around the mill wound a little river with forget-me-nots on its banks and apple-trees trailing their heavy branches almost into the stream.

After a year or two in the country Kate was sent back to London. Her father was a wood-engraver but he had not succeeded in business, so Mrs. Greenaway set up a shop to sell laces, children's dresses and fancy goods. Kate was sent now to an infants' school kept by a little old lady who wore a large, frilly cap, a frilly muslin dress, a scarf over her shoulders and a long apron. What a happy child she was, happier than either her brother or sisters, though they had the same surroundings. Her rich fancy found beauty everywhere.

The Greenaway children were allowed to roam about freely in the neighborhood of their home. They had given their promise to go no farther than a certain exciting corner and they always kept their word. But what streets those were through which they roamed! Where else were to be seen such grand, mysterious children guarded by their nurses, such rustling, perfumed ladies and such fascinating shop windows? And on that street corner, what adventures! Now a sailor man with a wooden leg appealed to the sympathy of passers by displaying a large, lurid picture of a ship overturned by a whale! Now, hark! a drum and the sound of a weird little shriek! A Punch and Judy show! Off the small Greenaways scamper to crowd around Mr. Punch. But alas! when their interest in the performance was at a white heat, just when the ghost was about to nab Mr. Punch, all too suddenly the manager would stop and declare he would not proceed a bit further unless he was paid with some pennies! Now the little Greenaways never had any pennies, and as the other small onlookers were frequently in the same plight, off would go Mr. Punch to more profitable fields, leaving black despair behind. But then, no use for long grieving! Punch was soon replaced by those fascinating mechanical puppets, the Fantoccini,—Mother Goose with her milk-pails from which jumped little children, the skelet-ton that came to bits and joined itself together again, and four little figures dancing a quadrille. Rarely was the corner unoccupied. There was always the chance of tumblers, tight-rope dancers, and that delightful street-organ, on top of which the ingeniously contrived figure of an executioner cut off the head of a queen about once every minute to the tune of the Marsellaise!

While Kate lived in London, her bedroom window looked out over naught more beautiful than red roofs and chimney pots but she used to imagine that steps led up from those roofs to a lovely garden where nasturtiums and flowers were blooming so near to the sky. She used to fancy, too, that a secret door had opened for her in the queer old houses that joined their own, and that that door led through lines of interesting old rooms, all so curious and delightful, and ending at last in a garden. By and by she began to want to express all this in painting, her love of children and of gardens, and so she set to work and studied to be a painter.

First, she painted designs for valentines and Christmas cards, then she illustrated books, and at last she wrote *Under the Window*, her very own book of rhymes, and drew its beautiful illustrations. Soon Kate Greenaway's fame spread around the world. The quaint little frocks and aprons, hats and breeches of her children, so funnily prim and neat, and yet so simple and graceful, set the style in dress for two continents. Dear, bright, quiet, little lady living in such seclusion! She showed people more of the charm of children's ways than they had ever dreamed of,—their graces, their thousand little prettinesses, and she left a pure love of childhood in many a heart that had never felt it before.

Marigold Garden *Under the Window* *Mother Goose*

GRIFFIS, WILLIAM ELLIOT (American, 1843–)
Dr. Griffis is a veteran of the Civil War and a great traveller who has made ten trips to Europe. In 1870, by invitation of the baron or damio of a province in Japan, he set out to organize schools there on American principles. He crossed America just after the completion of the trans-continental railway, when wild Indians on ponies, and soldiers at frontier forts still characterized the West. After twenty nine days on the Pacific on a sidewheel steamer, he spent seven weeks in Yedo and then went into the interior, the first American ever to have lived in a damio's capitol. On his return to Yedo, he crossed the country in mid-winter, often on snow-shoes, over the mountains, where wolves and wild boar roamed. After four years in Japan he returned to this country and became a minister. He has written Japanese, Korean, Dutch Belgian, Swiss and Welsh fairy tales.

GRIMM, WILHELM (1786–1859) and JACOB (1785–1863)
The first and most important collectors of German folk tales.

HALL, SARAH JOSEPHA (American, 1788–1879)

HARRIS, JOEL CHANDLER (American, 1848–1908)

A LITTLE, red-haired, freckle-faced midget of a boy dashing down the main street of a sleepy Georgia town behind a team of powerful horses and handling the reins with all the confidence of a six-foot hostler! Joel Chandler Harris, you mischievous little monkey! Come down off that box at once! Your mother is horrified.

It was well for Joel that he did not distress that good mother of his too often, for all her hopes were centered on him. Long years ago the boy's father had deserted the two and his mother had shouldered with splendid courage the burden of their support. She took in sewing and the two lived in a tiny cottage behind the great house of a friend.

Eatonton was a typical little Southern town of the days before

the Civil War. It had a courthouse and a town square, a tavern and several wide streets shaded by rows of fine old trees. On either side of the road, behind the trim boxwood hedges, rose stately colonial houses, the white pillars of their piazzas glinting here and there through the screen of odorous cedars, brightly blossoming myrtles and oleanders around them.

A fun-loving, rough-and-tumble lad on the surface was Joel, playing all sorts of pranks with his friends and rolling in the white mud gullies or munching ginger-cakes with the little negro children. But he was a tender-hearted boy at bottom and never forgot a kindness. See him now behind the old school house, showing a wren's nest to three little girls with such delight in the tiny, fragile thing. And how gentle and tender and kind the little girls are to the lad. A simple thing, but he never forgot it, never!

Now, at last, came the time when Joel must be up and doing! One day he found these words in a newspaper, "Boy Wanted to Learn the Printer's Trade." Here was his opportunity. He was only fourteen years old but he put away his tops and marbles, packed up his little belongings in an old-fashioned trunk, kissed his mother good-bye and was off. He went to work for Mr. Joseph Addison Turner of Turnwold, a fine old plantation, with cotton-fields white as snow in the season, and a group of negro cabins hid in a grove of oak trees behind the house. Mr. Turner published a paper called *The Countryman* and the little printing office where the boy worked was a primitive place, on the roof of which the squirrels scampered and the bluejays cracked their acorns. Not twenty steps from the office door a partridge had built her nest and was raising a brood of young, while more than once a red fox went loping stealthily by to the woods.

It was hard to say whether Joel enjoyed most the out-of-door life on the plantation, tramping about with a boy just his age who knew every path in the countryside, or browsing in Mr. Turner's fine library, for he dearly loved to read. But when the work and play of the day were ended, and the glow of the light-wood knot could be seen in the negro cabins, Joel and the Turner children would steal away from the house and visit their friends in the slave quarters. Tucked away in the nook of a chimney corner, Joel listened with eager interest while Old Harbert and Uncle George Terrell, their black faces a-gleam in the firelight, told their precious tales of Brer Rabbit and all the other lore of beasts and birds handed down from their African forefathers. And sometimes, while the yellow yam baked in the ashes, or a hoe-cake browned on the shovel, the negroes would croon a camp-meeting hymn, or sing a corn-shucking melody.

So passed months and years at Turnwold. And then the War! Joel Harris, a youth, with all the fire and passionate prejudices of boyhood, sitting up on a fence and watching the victorious Northern troops pass by, ploughing ankle-deep through the mud! The defeat of the South meant the end of *The Countryman* and the ruin of Mr. Turner. Joel had to start life anew. One paper after another gave him employment, and then, at last, he began to contribute to the *Atlanta Constitution* all those lively negro folk tales impressed so vividly on his mind in the old days at Turnwold—the stories of Uncle Remus. To Joel's immense surprise, Uncle Remus made him famous. And so it happened that the little red-haired boy, now grown a man with a wife and children of his own, could offer his mother a real home, and as his fame grew with the passing years, he brought her increasing happiness and fulfilled all her early dreams.

Uncle Remus, His Songs and Sayings *Daddy Jake, the Runaway* *The Tar Baby*

HARRISON, ELIZABETH (American, contemporary)

One of the founders of the National Kindergarten College.

Important Works:* *In Storyland

HAWTHORNE, NATHANIEL (American, 1804–1864)

THE solitary figure of a boy, alone on the top of a rocky cliff overlooking the sea at Salem. The surge beating up on the shore and the vast ocean stretching away forever, now grim and gray and angry, now flashing into light with the gleam of myriad jewels. HowNathaniel Hawthorne loved the sea! His father had been a sailor before he died and sailed far away—far, far away—to the Indies, to Africa and Brazil. Sometimes Nathaniel said to his mother that he, too, would go to sea and never, never return. A shy, solitary lad was Nathaniel, fond of his own fancies, fond of his own thoughts, fond of long, lonely rambles by the sea or through the queer little streets of Salem with their quaint old doorways and tragic memories of early witchcraft days.

When Nathaniel was fourteen his mother moved to a little town in Maine on the fresh, bright waters of Sebago Lake. Here the lad began again his solitary walks, exchanging the narrow streets of Salem for the boundless, tangled wilderness of Maine. He roamed the woods by day with his gun and rod, and in the moonlight nights of winter, skated upon the lake till midnight, alone, always alone. When he found himself far from home and wearied with exercise, he often took refuge in some wood-cutter's cabin, where half a tree would be burning upon the hearth.

But when Nathaniel grew up, he did not go to sea. He went to Bowdoin College, instead, where he met two young men who were destined to great distinction, Henry Wadsworth Longfellow and Franklin Pierce. While he was here certain new desires must have sprouted in his heart, for he wrote home to his mother, "How would you like some day to see a whole shelf full of books written by your son, with '*Hawthorne's Works*' printed on their backs?" And after graduating from Bowdoin, behold young Hawthorne sniffing no whiffs of old Ocean from behind the mast, but returned to Salem and writing, writing, writing, living in such seclusion, too, that even his own fellow citizens in the town where he was born scarcely knew him by sight!

Little money, however, came from his magazine articles even when these were published in book form as *Twice-told Tales*, and all too soon, life unrolled another picture,—Nathaniel now a weigher in the Customs House at Boston, measuring coal, salt and other bulky commodities that came in on foreign vessels, irksome employment, but for two years faithfully performed. Thereafter, Nathaniel doing a farm hand's chores at Brook Farm, striving with other earnest thinkers, to work out a way for men to lead better and simpler lives.

But in 1842 Hawthorne married and settled down in the handsome Old Manse at Concord. A beautiful place it was—the garden, the woods behind, and the river, to which he often fled to escape from too many visitors; and all his rich life there called forth a book which he named with tender affection *Mosses from an old Manse*.

In the years that followed Hawthorne moved about from place to place, but his powerful romance, *The Scarlet Letter*, settled once and for all the fact that he was a genius. In a little red wooden house at beautiful Lenox in the Berkshires he led an idyllic life of peace and joy, happy in the companionship of his wife and their three children. Their home stood in the midst of a broad valley that was like a great bowl flooded with golden sunshine. In the center there was a lake and all around, an amphitheatre of hills, about whose quiet peaks hung delicate purple mists like the softest of airy veils. Here Mr. Hawthorne would lie in the sunshine flecked with the shadows from a tree, and his little Una, Rose and Julian would climb over him and cover his chin and breast with long grass blades till he looked like Pan, the merry god of the woods, with a verdant woodland beard. He was constantly telling the children stories, too, and entered whole-heatedly into their play, for he was always far more at home with them than with their elders whom he avoided. At Lenox he wrote his *Wonder Book*, so loved by generations of children and his weird old story of Salem, *The House of the Seven Gables*.

In 1853 Hawthorne's college friend, now President Pierce, sent him to Liverpool as American Consul and for seven years he and his little family lived abroad. While visiting Rome and poking about into all its interesting old corners, or watching the moonlight silver the majestic Coliseum and the arches and fallen columns of the ancient Roman forum, he made a draft of a wonderful story of Rome to be known as *The Marble Faun*. When he returned once more to America, Hawthorne went to live at the house called The Wayside, in Concord, where he knew Louisa Alcott, Ralph Waldo Emerson, Henry Thoreau and all the other interesting Concord people. In that lovely spot he spent the rest of his days. Beautiful things were the children's stories that such a lover of children left to the world, but his novels are made of sterner stuff. They reveal with terrific force the fact that no man can disobey the still, small voice in his inmost soul that tells him when he is doing wrong, without the intensest suffering.

HEADLAND, ISAAC TAYLOR (American, 1859–)

Isaac Taylor Headland has been a missionary and professor at various universities in China, and a lecturer on Chinese art, life, and language in America. Once he heard a Chinese nurse repeating rhymes to a baby and determined to make a collection of Chinese nursery rhymes. A donkey driver who heard him repeating his precious rhyme, laughed and told him another one. Headland gave the man five cents and promised him as much more for each rhyme he could tell him. Soon he had nurses, drivers and children, all crowding to him to earn five cents by telling him nursery rhymes. Inside of a year he gathered six hundred, many of which are curious counterparts of our own Mother Goose.

HEPBURN, THOMAS N. "Gabriel Setoun" (Scotch, 1861–)

HERFORD, OLIVER (English-American, contemporary)

Important Works: Artful Anticks (whimsical verses).

HOGG, JAMES, "The Ettrick Shepherd" (Scotch, 1770–1835)

James Hogg was a Scotch shepherd who began to herd cows for a living when he was seven years old, and received for a half year's wages one ewe lamb and a pair of shoes! From his mother and the other shepherds the boy heard the old border ballads and stories of fairies and giants, but at the age of twenty he still could not write all the alphabet. The remaining letters he studied out from a book in order that he might write down a few simple verses that he had been making. It chanced then that someone recited to him the poem of *Tam O'Shanter* and told him the story of Burns, the ploughman poet. That was sufficient to make the young shepherd resolve to be likewise a poet. One day while he was driving his sheep into Edinburgh he was seized with a sudden desire to see his verses in print. At once he sat down on a stone and scribbled them off on paper. Then he hurried on to a publisher and induced him to put them in print. These ballads attracted the attention of Sir Walter Scott, and through his kindness the Ettrick shepherd soon gained some renown. But though he now had a farm of his own, he still retained his simple, rough, peasant ways. Once he said to Scott," Ye can never suppose that I belong to your school o' chivalry. Ye are the King o' that school, but I'm King o' the mountain and fairy school which is far higher than yours!" Indeed, his best poems are always of fairies. When he stepped outside that charmed fairy ring, his music and magic vanished.

HOLLAND, JOSIAH GILBERT (American, 1819–1881)

The founder of *Scribner's Monthly*, now the *Century Magazine*.

HOOD, THOMAS (English poet, 1799–1845)

HOWELLS, WILLIAM DEAN (American, 1837–1920)

For years the editor of *The Atlantic Monthly* and founder of that school of writers which portrays commonplace American life.

Important Works: The Flight of Pony Baker. Christmas Every Day.

INGELOW, JEAN (English, 1820–1897)

Important Works: Mopsa, the Fairy. Stories Told to a Child

IRVING, WASHINGTON (American, 1783–1859)

LONG, long ago, just at the close of the American Revolution, when New York was a little old town with all the air of an overgrown village, a small boy was born there whose mother named him Washington Irving in honor of General Washington. When the little fellow was about six years old his nurse took him one day to see the procession escorting General Washington to Federal Hall to take his oath as first President of the United States. Pressing through the throng, the nurse dragged her small charge straight up to the great man and told him that the boy had been given his name. With a kindly smile Washington stopped to give his young namesake his blessing.

Washington Irving grew to be an adventurous lad. He liked to visit new scenes and observe strange manners and customs. When he was still the merest slip of a child he made long tours of discovery into foreign parts, the foreign parts of his own little city, and more than once his parents had to employ the town-crier to hunt up their wandering son by crying his name through the town. He loved to roam around the Battery, and to wander out on the piers to watch the out-going ships departing to distant climes. With what longing eyes did he gaze after their lessening sails and waft himself in fancy to the very ends of the earth. As he grew into boyhood, Washington extended the range of his observations. He now spent his holiday afternoons in rambles far out into the country round about New York, visiting the little villages where the descendants of the old Dutch settlers continued to dwell, and pushing on, on to the very distant hills. He made voyages too, in a sail-boat up the lordly Hudson River whose cliffs and towering highlands breathed forth the very spirit of old Dutch and Indian legends. He penetrated into the heart of the

Catskill Mountains, that rise to the west of the river, changing their magical hues with every hour of the day.

At times he peered into some dark glen, lonely and wild and tangled, or stood at the foot of a waterfall, a sliding sheet of silver, slipping down over mossy rocks, again he came out on the edge of a precipice, whence he could look out for miles and miles over all the sun-flooded valley and see far down below the twisting ribbon of the Hudson. He knew those mountains in sunshine and in storm—now in the calm of evening when they threw their long blue shadows so peacefully over the valleys, or gathered a hood of gray vapors about their heads to glow in the setting sun like a crown of glory—now when the thunderclouds lowered, the lightning went leaping from crag to crag and peal after peal of thunder rolled crashing down their heights. And at the foot of these fairy mountains, its smoke curling up through the trees, would nestle a little Dutch village, where the houses had latticed windows and the gable fronts were surmounted by the quaintest of weathercocks. Here in the shade of some great tree before the old tavern, Irving could always find a club of worthies smoking their pipes and whiling away the long, lazy summer's day by telling endless stories.

But as the boy grew to young manhood, he began to long to go further still in his travels. He had seen and loved so much of the natural beauty of America, her mighty lakes and mountains, her valleys and trackless forests, her broad, deep rivers and boundless plains, but now old Europe beckoned him. He longed for her treasures of art, her quaint and different customs, her poetic associations. He longed to loiter about her ruinous old castles, and reconstruct in his fancy all the shadowy grandeur of her past. And so when the young maid who had been his sweetheart died and there was nothing more to hold him in America, off he went to England. Already he was known there as the author of *Salmagundi Papers* and that humorous mixture of fact and fancy, *Knickerbocker's History of New York*. And so in England he found a place ready made for him. He could travel now as much as he pleased and he set down in his *Sketch Book* all the interesting things he saw—little home scenes of rural repose and sheltered quiet, peasants in country lanes, as well as the solemn magnificence of grand old Westminster Abbey.

A journey to Spain gave him the rich store of Spanish and Moorish legend to put into two books, *The Alhambra* and *The Conquest of Granada*. Here, too, he came across certain intensely interesting documents concerning Columbus which had heretofore been unknown and what must he do but write a wonderful *Life of Columbus*. After seventeen long years abroad, he returned at length to New York and bought the beautiful place called Sunnyside at Tarrytown on the Hudson, not far from Sleepy Hollow. No woman ever replaced the sweetheart of his youth and Irving never married, but here at beautiful Sunnyside he passed all the rest of his days, quitting it only once for any length of time, and then to serve for four years as American Minister to Spain. But however great was the volume of work that Washington Irving put forth, his name always calls first to mind the magic of the Catskills and the Hudson, gleaming through mists of romantic old Dutch legends.

Important Works: The Legend of Sleepy Hollow. Rip Van Winkle.

JACKSON, HELEN HUNT (American, 1831–1885)

Helen Hunt Jackson once heard two Indians in Boston tell the tale of their people's wrongs at the hands of the American government and she was so moved that she wrote first a pamphlet and then the story of *Ramona* to arouse the public to demand reforms.

Important Works: Nelly's Silver Mine. Ramona. Cat Stories.

JACOBS, JOSEPH (English editor, born in Australia, 1854–)

Important Works: English Fairy Tales. Celtic Fairy Tales. Indian Fairy Tales.

JEWETT, SARAH ORNE (American, 1849–1909)

A Maine woman who wrote very truthful New England stories.

Important Works: The Country of the Pointed Firs. Betty Leicester. Deephaven.

JOHNSON, CLIFTON (American, editor of fairy tales 1865–)

Important Works: The Oak Tree Fairy Book. The Birch Tree Fairy Book.

JORDAN, DAVID STARR (American, 1851–)

Dr. Jordan is a big, simple, warm-hearted, impetuous man whose chief work of late years has been the attempt to impress men with a sense of the uselessness of war. He grew up on a farm in New York and worked his way through college by waiting on table, husking corn and digging ditches. He became the first president of Leland Stanford University and is a scientist of renown.

Important Works: The Book of Knight and Barbara. True Tales of Birds and Beasts.

KEATS, JOHN (English, 1795—1821)

John Keats was a small boy whose father kept a livery stable in London, but he was given a good education and proved a studious little fellow. Indeed, his masters had to drive him away from his books to get him to play out of doors. Books! Books! Books! He carried them with him everywhere, even to the dining table and fought valiantly if he was disturbed in his reading. A high spirited lad he was and always easily moved to deep feeling. Once he fought for an hour with a butcher's boy whom he found tormenting a kitten. In the lad's heart there dwelt, too, a deep love of beauty. The wild beauty and color of the Cornish Coast—how he loved it! All nature to him was a poem—the wind in the trees was music! Once he visited the British Museum and saw there the lovely old relics of Greek and Roman life. Presto! there sprang into life in his heart all that interest in Greek subjects to be shown later in his poems. Keats was educated to be a surgeon but friendship for the poets, Shelley and Leigh Hunt, soon turned all his thoughts to poetry. His volumes of verse, however, were violently criticised and at length the young poet, sick and disappointed, went off to Italy where he died. Then only was he recognized as among England's greatest poets.

KILMER, JOYCE (American, 1886–1918)

An active young fellow, full of mirth and keen zest in life was Joyce Kilmer. When the World War began he was already a poet of renown. He enlisted immediately and was killed in action.

KINGSLEY, CHARLES (English, 1818–1875)

ON the rocky coast of Devonshire lies the queer little fishing village of Clovelly that goes tumbling down from the top of the cliff to the bright blue waters of the bay below, its little cobble stone street so steep that mules can scarcely climb it, and its tiny white cottages clinging, goodness knows how! to the rock, each peering curiously over the roof of the one below. In Clovelly a group of old fishermen may always be found, sunning themselves on benches, looking far out to sea and telling wild tales of the ocean. Here the rector's small son, Charles Kingsley, used often to come to hear the old tars tell their stories, and the life of the hardy fishermen, their toils and dangers stirred him deeply. All Devonshire—its moors and fens, its fragrant country lanes—Charles Kingsley loved it all.

But by and by, young Charles had to leave his beloved and beautiful Devonshire and go to King's College in London. How he hated life in the city! Often he dreamed of leaving the University and going to America to be a trapper and hunter in the west. Just then, however, he fell deeply in love with a certain young lady whose parents could not welcome a penniless student. So he made haste to finish his schooling and became the curate of Eversley.

Full of boyish fun and overflowing vitality was the young curate of Eversley though he was deeply religious too, and worked with tireless enthusiasm. Everybody loved him and he loved everybody, the poor and oppressed most of all. Presently he began to write pamphlets and books on all the great topics that stirred men's minds in his day, and so vigorously did he write that his influence spread far beyond the limits of his parish. Slowly he rose to be one of the great men of his time, Canon of Westminster and Chaplain to Queen Victoria. But the very best of his books are certain stories astir with the adventurous spirit of old Clovelly days.

Important Works: Water Babies. The Heroes. (Greek Fairy Tales.) Westward Ho!

LA FONTAINE, JEAN DE (French poet, 1621–1695)

Fables in Rhyme, illustrated by John Rae. La Fontaine's Fables, illustrated by Boutet de Monvel.

LAGERLÖF, SELMA (Swedish, 1858–)

IN the pretty rectory at Marbacka Manor in the beautiful province of Varmland in Sweden there once lived a little girl. The rectory was a lovely place, sweet with laughter and peaceful joys, with love of books and people. As a little girl, Selma Lagerlöf preferred reading or imagining stories to out-of-door sports. She often played theatre with her brothers and sisters and it was always Selma who hung up the quilts and blankets to make the stage, dressed up the little actors and told them how to say their parts. At Marbacka Manor Selma lived for twenty years, reading, writing, and dreaming that sometime a stranger would come to her gate and bring her fame by publishing her stories.

But by and by the pretty old rectory was sold and Selma had to go to Stockholm to teach school. One day it flashed upon her like a blinding light that she must write a story of the Varmland, of the people and country she knew so well. So she began the *Saga of Gösta Berling*. But she wrote so slowly, slowly. It was years before the first chapter was finished. Then one day a prize was offered by a magazine for the best novelette and Selma's sister urged her to complete the first five chapters of her story. Not only did she win the prize but the magazine offered to publish the book if she would complete it at once. Accordingly, a friend, gave her enough money to free her from the necessity to teach and in a year she completed the work. *Gösta Berling* brought her fame and fortune and enabled her to buy back her dear old home in Varmland.

In 1908 the school authorities invited Selma Lagerlöf to write a book for the schools which should keep in the hearts of the young people of today the old folk-lore and history of Sweden and teach them the geography and the natural history of their country. The results were *The Wonderful Adventures of Nils* and *Further Adventures of Nils,* books which are classics in every country, and won for Selma the Nobel prize, the world's greatest prize for literature.

LARCOM, LUCY (American, 1826–1893)

A girl who worked in the mills at Lowell, Mass. and wrote for the mill worker's magazine. Later the editor of *Our Young Folks*.

LAZARUS, EMMA (American, 1849–1887)

Emma Lazarus was a young Jewish girl, shy and sensitive, who lived in a world of poetry and books and published her first volume of verse when she was fifteen, sombre, tragic poems breathing the tragic spirit of her race. She worshiped Emerson and he was her literary adviser, writing her what books to study. After the anti-Jewish outrages in Russia and Germany in 1881, she threw herself heart and soul into the movement against such barbarism. Not only did she write poetry in a crusade of protest but she worked untiringly among the terror-stricken immigrants who flocked into this country. Such a woman could well understand what America meant as a land of promise to the poor and oppressed of Europe.

LEAR, EDWARD (English, 1812–1888)

Lear's *Nonsense Rhymes* with their comic pictures are child classics.

LINDSAY, MAUD (American kindergarten worker, 1874–)

Important Works: Mother Stories. More Mother Stories. Story Garden for Little Children.

LINDSAY, NICHOLAS VACHELL (American, 1879–)

A young boy from Springfield, Illinois, once dreamed an exciting dream of an old fashioned battle between armored men. He jumped out of bed at once and wrote the dream down in a poem called *The Battle*. But the next morning his poem seemed so much less interesting than his dream that he had to help it out by drawing a picture! When the same poet-artist began, however, to write verse in earnest in New York he found no market for his poems. Accordingly, he decided that the common man must learn to reverence beauty before beauty could succeed in America. With only a bundle of songs for his fortune, he left New York and tramped through eight states, begging food and lodgings as he went and reciting his poems in return, preaching the gospel of beauty to the farmer, the most worth while element, he believed, in American life.

Important Works: The Congo. The Chinese Nightingale

THE LATCH KEY

LONGFELLOW, HENRY WADSWORTH (1807–1882.)

IN an historic old wooden house, overshadowed by splendid elms and standing on one of the spacious streets of Cambridge, that delightful old university town, there lived once a modest, deep-hearted gentleman whose highest ambition was to be a perfect man and through sympathy and love to help others to be the same. The old house had been built before the Revolution and occupied by Washington when he took command of the American army in 1776. Its study windows looked across the green Brighton meadows far away to the Brookline hills. It was in that study just at twilight that the poet used to hear the patter of little feet in the room above him and see, in the lamplight, his children on the stairs. A rush and a raid from the doorway, they were swarming over his chair—Alice, laughing Allegra and "Edith with golden hair."

A scholar and a poet was Longfellow, a Professor at Harvard University, and yet he always seemed to have time for everybody and everything. Never was he too busy to see a caller, or to help by word or deed whoever was in distress. Often strangers called to see him, or children, not venturing to call, hung about his garden gate, hoping just to catch a glimpse of him. To such his courtesy was complete. He never seemed to think they had come for a peep at him, but took it for granted that they wanted to see Washington's study, which he showed them with simple pleasure. Indeed, far from trying to hide himself from intruders, he rarely even drew the blinds of his study windows at night. What a sunny, genial nature was his, full of courage, tenderness and strength. In joy and sorrow, he lived life beautifully and happily, with neither envy nor malice and with unbounded charity.

Through his mother Longfellow was descended from John Alden and Priscilla, those precious Puritan lovers whose quaint courtship he described so beautifully in *Miles Standish*. In his boyhood he lived amid the quiet surroundings of Portland, Maine, where he was born, and he never forgot the pleasant streets of that dear old town, the shadowy lines of trees which permit, here and there through their branches, a sudden glimpse of the sea. He never forgot

"the black wharves and the slips,
And the sea-tides tossing free,
And Spanish sailors with bearded lips,
And the beauty and mystery of the ships,
And the magic of the sea."

His college days at Bowdoin, where he was a classmate of Hawthorne, introduced him to the falls of the Androscoggin River, wild scenery and rich in Indian lore and legend. The greater part of his life, however, was spent at Cambridge, writing and teaching, quiet days and little varied save for frequent trips to Europe. He was a poet of the past, of legendary heroes, and not like Lowell, a moulder of the present, but the music and deep feeling in his work have made him more beloved than any other American poet.

Important Works: Hiawatha. The Courtship of Miles Standish. Evangeline.

LOTHROP, (MARGARET SIDNEY) American 1844–

Important Works: The Five Little Peppers and How They Grew.

LOWELL, AMY (American, 1874–)

Amy Lowell holds a high rank among the modern school of poets for her imagery, color, power and vivid characterization.

LOWELL, JAMES RUSSELL (American, 1819–1891)

The foremost American poet in expressing the ideals of the early American republic, and the first editor of *The Atlantic Monthly*.

MacDONALD, GEORGE (Scotch, 1824–1905)

George MacDonald was a minister, teacher and writer who kept through life the heart of a child. He was deeply religious, though not in the conventional way, and had a heart overflowing with charity for all. Though he was never very well off and had a family of eleven children of his own, he frequently added to it by adopting children in need, and his most enduring work has proved to be his beautiful children's stories.

At the Back of the North Wind. The Princess and Curdie. The Princess and the Goblin.

MARE, WALTER DE LA (English poet, 1873–)

MARKHAM, CHARLES EDWIN (American, 1852–)

A LITTLE five year old boy once went from Oregon City to live with his widowed mother and deaf and dumb brother on a lonely ranch in California. Here the boy worked at farming, blacksmithing, herding, and when he earned twenty dollars for ploughing a neighbor's field, he bought himself some books. But his mother was a stern, hard woman, who cared little about his education, so at length the boy ran away from home to work with a band of threshers, nor would he return until his mother promised to let him work his way through school. In college Markham supported himself by teaching freshman classes while doing sophomore and junior work, and he and four other students lived in a bare room under the college bell-tower, cooking their own meals, which consisted chiefly of beans! When he began writing verse for the California papers he found success and later did newspaper work in New York. His best known poem is *The Man with the Hoe.*

MASEFIELD, JOHN (English 1878–)

AS a small boy Masefield used to run away from home, sometimes for days at a time, so at last his father sent him to sea to work off his surplus energy aboard a merchant vessel. For ten years he lived on the ocean and gained there that love of ships and the sea which colors all his work. But when he was sixteen he left the ship at New York with five dollars and a chest of clothes, fired now with desire to study. He worked on a farm, in a bakery, in a hotel, and in a carpet factory, but every Friday on pay day he went to the book store and bought books. Then the day came when he began to write. He has written stirring narrative poems and splendid stories of adventure.

Important Works: Martin Hyde, the Duke's Messenger. Jim Davis. Voyages of Discovery.

MEREDITH, GEORGE (English novelist, 1822–1909)

MILLER, JOAQUIN (Cincinnatus Heine Miller) 1841–1913.

A prairie schooner in early pioneer days, toiling westward, westward, across the desert, across the Rockies, across the Sierras; and in the lumbering old wagon among his elders, a small boy named Cincinnatus Heine Miller. The boy's family were on their way from Indiana where he had been born, to settle in Oregon. The very spirit of the West seemed to breathe itself into that boy, the free breezy spirit of America's great western plains, where there is "room, room to turn round in, to breathe and be free,"

"And to east and to west, to the north and the sun,
Blue skies and brown grasses are welded as one,
And the buffalo come, like a cloud on the plain,
Pouring on like the tide of a storm-driven main,
And the lodge of the hunter to friend and to foe
Offers rest; and unquestioned you come and you go."

Young Cincinnatus was often in need of money so he once set out sturdily from home and joined a wood-cutters' camp. There the small urchin was found by his elders chopping away at a great rate, nor would he return until he had earned what he set out to get. Later he joined the gold-miners in California and for five years he lived among the Pacific Coast Indians. In Canyon City, Colorado, where he practiced law, he met a certain Mexican bandit named Joaquin (Walk-in) whose name struck him as so much more picturesque and interesting than his own that he cast away Cincinnatus Heine forever and henceforth called himself Joaquin. Soon he published a volume of western poems called *Joaquin et al* but it was when he went to London a few years later that the big breezy westerner made his first great success with *Songs of the Sierras*. England grew most enthusiastic and feted him everywhere. At all festivities he appeared in a flannel shirt and sombrero!

In a beautiful retreat called "The Heights" on the crest of a mountain in California he passed the later years of his life. Here he lived in good old western simplicity with his mother and a few friends, the best loved writer of the West, the Poet of the Sierras.

Important Works: True Bear Stories.

MILTON, JOHN (English, 1608–1674)

John Milton was a stern old Puritan, a born rebel from his boyhood, an apostle of liberty, who hated tyranny and was yet neither gracious nor tender. He was Secretary for Foreign Tongues to Oliver Cromwell, the Puritan Protector of England, and during that work became totally blind. But with his tremendous power and force he never gave up his work. Out under the trees in his garden he forced his three daughters to read to him hour after hour, long, tiresome books of which they often understood nothing.

With Cromwell's death and the return of the Royalists to power, Milton lost his standing and was forced for a time to go into hiding. His books against the Royalist cause were publicly burnt and he himself was thrown into prison. When he was released, he was a friendless old man, blind as well, but with that tremendous spirit of his he set to work once again and finished the most powerful of all his works, one of the greatest epic poems in the English language—*Paradise Lost*, as well as two other long poems.

NEKRASSOV, NIKOLAI ALEXEIEVITCH (Russian, 1821–78)

Nekrassov was one of the early patriots of Russia who dared to speak out against the tyranny and oppression of the Czar. His mother was a gentle Polish woman who gave her whole life to teaching him, instilling into him, heart and soul, the love of simple, kindly things. This made him hate all the more the ugly punishments he saw when he went on trips with his father, a brutal Russian officer and Chief of District Police. When Nikolai refused to be a soldier his father disinherited him. For three years he worked his way through college, hungry day and night, but at last by his ceaseless efforts he made a place for himself in the literary world and rose to be Editor of Russia's foremost magazine. Through his vivid pen-pictures of all types of Russian life, he led young Russia to hate oppression, to understand the various classes of their own country, especially the working class, and to love freedom.

NESBIT, EDITH (English writer of children's stories, 1858–)

NEWELL, PETER (American, 1862–)

One of the most original of humorists, whose drawings of funny little round-eyed children exactly fit his funny little verses.

Pictures and Rhymes. The Top Turveys. The Slant Book.

NOEL, THOMAS (English poet, 1799–1861)

NOYES, ALFRED (English, 1880–)

One of the foremost English poets of the present day. He was born in Staffordshire and educated at Oxford. In 1913 he gave a course of lectures in Boston on *The Sea in English Poetry* and was, for the next three years, visiting professor at Princeton University.

PAINE, ALBERT BIGELOW (American, 1861–)

Albert Bigelow Paine was born in New Bedford, Maine and educated at Xenia, Illinois. He began writing for the Kansas newspapers while living in Fort Scott, and from there went to New York. He has been a department editor of *St. Nicholas* and has written many delightful stories for children.

Important Works: The Arkansaw Bear. Hollow Tree and Deep Woods Book.

PERRAULT, CHARLES (French, 1628–1703)

A courtly French author who made the first collection of French Fairy Tales which he called *Tales of Mother Goose*. These were not the jingles, but the stories of Cinderella, The Sleeping Beauty, etc.

POE, EDGAR ALLAN (American, 1809–1849)

A great American poet and writer of short stories, but of an eccentric genius, dark and unhappy.

POULSSON, ANNE EMILIE (1853–)

Miss Poulsson is a prominent kindergarten worker.

Important Works: Father and Baby Plays. The Runaway Donkey. Through the Farmyard Gate

PRENTISS, ELIZABETH (American, 1818–1878)

PRINGLE, THOMAS (Scotch, 1789–1834)

A Scotch writer who made an interesting trip to Africa.

PYLE, HOWARD (American, 1853–1911)

A SMALL boy once lay on the rug before the fire in a certain house in Wilmington, Delaware, while his mother read him *Robinson Crusoe.* Vividly he pictured to himself all the interesting history of that venturesome hero as he tramped about on his lonely island with the savage, Friday. Sometimes Howard Pyle's mother read him *Gulliver's Travels, Tanglewood Tales, Ivanhoe* or the *Arabian Nights,* but whatever she read, he always lay there and saw pictures, pictures, pictures. Often he tried to put these pictures down in drawing. Indeed, his mother inspired him early with a love of all beautiful things—particularly pictures and books. Once when he was a very tiny boy he felt himself so moved to write a poem that he called for paper and pencil and was sitting with paper on knee all ready to write before he ever stopped to think that he did not yet know how to read nor to make a single letter! Keen was young Howard's disappointment.

Rather than go to college when he grew up, Howard Pyle went to an art school where his ability to make pictures was trained. Since he so dearly loved pictures in books he began making illustrations and soon he was both writing and illustrating his own stories. How he loved a quaint old picturesque tale of adventure, whether of knights or of pirates, and he left boys and girls many tales of both, illustrated with vigor and a keen love of color and beauty, for Howard Pyle was one of America's foremost illustrators.

The Garden Behind the Moon. The Merry Adventures of Robin Hood. Men of Iron. The Wonder Clock. Otto of the Silver Hand. Stolen Treasure. Pepper and Salt.

KATHERINE PYLE (American contemporary)

Katherine Pyle is the sister of Howard Pyle and is herself an author and artist of unusual merit.

As the Goose Flies. The Christmas Angel. Careless Jane. Fairy Tales from Many Lands.

RAMÉE, LOUISE DE LA (1859–1908)

Once there was a little girl living in France, the child of a French father and an English mother. When she began trying to say her own name, Louisa, she could call herself nothing but "Ouida." Little did she or her parents dream then that she was going to make that name of Ouida famous. When she was twenty she left France and went to England where she began at once to write stories. Her romances were extravagant, sentimental and impossible things but they were wildly popular and they made her a large fortune. Then off went Miss Ouida to live in Italy in such fashion as she deemed fitting for a wealthy and famous young novelist. Tales are told of how she rode through the streets of Florence in a coach lined with sky-blue leather, wearing an orange colored dress and black lace mantilla. Poor, foolish, little lady. In spite of her great success and her many fine qualities she was helpless, vain, and unbusinesslike and her last years found her in poverty, deserted by all save a few dumb pets of which she was always passionately fond. Her only work of real value is that written for children.

Important Works: The Dog of Flanders. The Nuremberg Stove. Bimbi. Moufflou

RANDS, WILLIAM BRIGHTY (English, 1823–1880)

RANSOME, ARTHUR (English, contemporary)

RICHARDS, LAURA E. (American, contemporary)

Daughter of Julia Ward Howe and a noted writer for children.

Important Works: Captain January. The Joyous Story of Toto. The Golden Windows.

RILEY, JAMES WHITCOMB (American, 1853–1916)

James Whitcomb Riley is the beloved poet of Indiana, the Hoosier poet, who has written so many homely, heartfelt things of and for the people, in their own simple style and idiom. He worked first as a sign painter, then joined a company of strolling players for whom he wrote songs and plays. Later he was one of the editors of the *Indianapolis Journal*. A genuine poet of childhood was Riley, too, full of deep love and sympathy for children.

A Host of Children (Riley's child rhymes illustrated in color)

*ROOSEVELT, THEODORE (American, 1858–1919)

A sturdy young fellow, alert and energetic of movement, his spectacles gleaming in the sun, was making his way on a tough little western pony toward Chimney Butte Ranch on the Little Missouri River in the Bad Lands of North Dakota. All around him the country was bare, wild and desolate, vast stretches of bleak prairie, parched by the scorching sun and varied only by abrupt and savage hills called by the cowboys buttes. It was a land of enormous distances, stretching away forever, with no farms and no fences, only at wide intervals little log ranch houses with mud roofs where lived the ranchmen whose herds ranged over the prairie. In the fertile river bottoms hundreds of long-horned cattle grazed while cowboys dashed recklessly among them on half-broken ponies. No soft loveliness in such a scene, only a wild, stark, bold and rugged beauty that made it a fit background for the bold and rugged men who lived and worked there. Such a scene had a strange appeal for Theodore Roosevelt. He loved it; vigorous outdoor life in that wild country thrilled him; he wanted to feel himself the comrade of the men who lived there. And so a year ago he had bought Chimney Butte Ranch. Queer! A New Yorker of a wealthy old Dutch family, who had lived all his life in an aristocratic section of New York and was a graduate of Harvard University into the bargain, choosing such a primitive life of toil and hardship, and queerer still that the rough plainsmen should overcome their prejudice against Eastern "dudes", and love and admire Theodore Roosevelt. Back in New York a great sorrow had just befallen the young man, the loss of his wife, and he had come out to Dakota to fling himself heart and soul into the work of the ranch and forget his grief in activity.

It was over at Elkhorn Ranch that Roosevelt now kept most of his stock. One day he had followed the Little Missouri River

***Read *The Boy's Life of Roosevelt* by Hermann Hagedorn**

forty miles north of Chimney Butte where it takes a long swing westward through a fertile bottom bordered by sheer cliffs. There on a low bluff surmounted by cottonwood trees he found the interlocked antlers of two great elk and he decided that this was a better place for his ranch than Chimney Butte. So he and his men had driven the cattle over and taken possession of the rude little shack already built there. It was a company of quiet, bronzed, self-reliant men with whom Roosevelt had surrounded himself out there in the West. There were Joe Ferris and Joe and Sylvaine Merrifield, seasoned plainsmen who were in charge of Chimney Butte Ranch when he first came out and hunted buffalo with them a year before. And there were the two backwoodsmen from Maine, whom Roosevelt had gone east to fetch, Bill Sewall and his nephew, Will Dow. Bill Sewall was a character. Roosevelt had learned to know and love him in his Harvard days when he went up to Lake Mattawamkeag to hunt in the Maine wilderness. A stalwart, vigorous man with an indomitable spirit was Sewall, the sort of man who could hew down with his axe forty or fifty giants of the forest in one day, who gloried in the conflict with wind and storm and was the happiest in his canoe on Mattawamkeag when the waves were highest, exulting in his strength and bidding the elements defiance. This man was all his life long one of Roosevelt's closest friends.

In the fall, when everything was well settled at Elkhorn, Roosevelt set out for a round-up in the great cattle country west of the Little Missouri. The search for stray cattle took him and his party across southeastern Montana and halfway across Wyoming to the very base of the Big Horn Mountains, where eight years before General Custer had been killed by the Indians. Those mountains tempted Roosevelt. The work of rounding up cattle was now well over so he and Merrifield took a pack-train and leaving their canvas covered wagon with the rest of the party, they started up into the mountains. Along an old Indian trail through dense pine woods and up the sides of rocky gorges they ascended—up and up

and up, driving their pack-train with endless difficulty over fallen timber and along the edge of dizzy precipices. At length they camped in a beautiful glade surrounded by pine trees, pitching their tents beside a clear running mountain brook. From here they hunted among the peaks round about. The weather was clear and cold with thin ice covering the mountain tarns and now and again light falls of snow made the forest gleam in the moonlight. Through the frosty air they could often hear the far-off musical note of the bull-elk calling. Roosevelt loved the adventure of the chase, but he loved even more the majesty of the trees and the companionship of all the shy wild creatures that sprang across his path. What alluring glimpses he caught of the inner life of the mountains. But when indeed he set out to hunt, he pursued his aim with dogged persistence. He might be sobbing for breath and with sweat streaming into his eyes but if he was after an elk, after an elk he continued to be in spite of all misadventures until he got one; if his aim was a grizzly he kept on the warpath and never rested until the grizzly was his. Certainly Theodore Roosevelt never avoided difficulties. He pressed on determinedly through them, and made difficulties contribute to his success.

After some days in the mountains the two men at length rejoined their wagon and started on the three hundred mile journey home. It was long and weary travelling, galloping beside the lumbering wagon over the desolate prairie. After many days they reached a strange and romantic region—isolated buttes of sandstone cut by the weather into curious caves and columns, battlements and spires. A beautiful and fantastic place it was, and here they made their camp. Soon the flame of their camp fire went leaping up the cliffs till those weird and solemn shapes seemed to writhe into life. Outside the circle of the firelight the cliffs shone silver beneath a great full moon and threw grotesque black shadows across the dusky plain. But, the next morning, all was changed, a gale was blowing and the rain came beating down. A miserable day and night followed and then another. Not until the third day dawned could they start on their way again. That night they camped by a dry creek in a broad bottom covered with thick parched grass. To make sure that their camp fire should not set the surrounding grass alight, they burned a circle clear, standing about with branches to keep the flames in check. Suddenly a puff of wind! The fire leapt up and roared like a beast as it raced along the plain. In five minutes the whole bottom would be ablaze. The men fought furiously. Hair and eyebrows were singed black, but they kept on fighting until the flames were subdued.

At this time they were still three days from home as the crawling team would make the journey, so Roosevelt concluded after supper that night to press on ahead of the wagon with Merrifield and ride the full distance before dawn. At nine o'clock they saddled the tough little ponies they had ridden all day and rode off out of the circle of firelight, loping mile after mile beneath the moon and the stars. Now and again bands of antelope swept silently by them and once a drove of cattle charged past, dark figures that set the ground rumbling beneath their heavy tread. The first glow of the sun was touching the level bluffs of Chimney Butte into light as they galloped into the valley of the Little Missouri.

Winter was hard at Chimney Butte that year as always. There was little snow but the cold was fierce in its intensity. The trees cracked and groaned from the strain of the frost and even the stars seemed to snap and glitter. The river lay frozen fast and wolves and lynxes travelled up and down it at night as though it had been a highway. Roosevelt lived chiefly now at Chimney Butte writing somewhat on books he had started and reading much but sharing, too, all the hardships of the winter work. It was not pleasant to be out of doors in the biting wind but the herds had to be watched. The cattle suffered much and stood in shivering groups huddled together in the shelter of the canyons. Every day for Roosevelt began with breakfast at five o'clock, three hours before sunrise, and from then until dark he or his men were almost constantly in the saddle, riding about among the cattle and turning back any that seemed to be straggling away toward the open plain.

During the severest weather there were fifty new-bought and decidedly refractory ponies to be broken. Day after day in the icy cold Roosevelt labored patiently in the corral among them. More than once he was bucked by his steed in the presence of a gallery of grinning cowboys, but in the end it was noteworthy that it was always the pony and not Roosevelt who was broken!

In the late Spring the men built a new ranch house at Elkhorn, plain but comfortable and homelike. Then Will Dow went back east to Maine and returned with a newly married bride of his own and with Bill Sewall's wife and little three year old daughter. These women were backwoodswomen, self-reliant, fearless, high hearted as their mates. What with their cheery voices, their thinking of this and that to make life more pleasant, their baking and putting all things in order at the ranch, they soon turned the house into a real home. Now began happy days at Elkhorn, days of elemental toil and hardship, and of strong, elemental pleasures, rest after labor, food after hunger, warmth and shelter after bitter cold. No room here for social distinctions. Each respected and loved the other because each knew the other to be steadfast, loyal and true. Roosevelt saddled his own horse, fed the pigs and now and then washed his own clothes. Through the cold evenings he loved to stretch himself out at full length on the elk hides and wolf skins before the great fireplace while the blazing logs cracked and roared. Doubtless he often thought back then on his own life.

What an alert, energetic, enthusiastic, little fellow he had been, frail in body originally, for he had acquired that tough physique of his only through persistent facing of hardships. His first deep interest had been in natural history. O that Museum of Natural History he had founded at the age of nine! And the treatise he had written in a two-for-a-nickel note book, "*Natural History on Insects*" wherein with the most picturesque spelling he wrote of "beetlles","misqueto hawks", ants, etc. all whose "habbits" he declared he had gained from his own "ofservation". He had pursued the study of natural history with an almost ruthless singleness of purpose, just as he did all things all through life. If it seemed to him necessary for his studies that he keep a few dead field mice in the family refrigerator he did so, if he felt obliged to have a snake or two in the guest room water pitcher, that he did likewise. For a few years, whether in America, or in Europe, or journeying up the Nile with his parents, his brother and sister, he had the one single aim of chasing down specimens for his study. And he never lost that interest in natural history, but gradually there began to awake in him deeper interests and stirring dreams. He was thrilled by the heroes of the old epics. He wanted to be like them. He wanted to be of the company of the doers of deeds, men who faced life and death calmly with clear eyes and did not rate life too highly in the balance with what they deemed justice. And gradually he became more and more deeply aware of the struggle it is to translate dreams into reality. He saw ever more clearly that men attain only through endless struggle against the sloth, the love of ease, the impurities, the doubts and fears of their own hearts. But every aspiration in him reached out to be one with whose who throughout all ages have fought the battles of Right against Wrong and he determined to build up for himself a clean, valiant, fighting soul.

When he was graduated from college he decided that the real fighters of his day were the men who went into politics and used their weapons there in behalf of Justice and Fair Play, so he deliberately joined the Twenty-fifth District Republican Association.

"But politics are so low" said his aristocratic friends with their noses in the air. "And political organizations are not controlled by gentlemen, but by saloon keepers, street car conductors and the like!" "Very well," replied Theodore with emphasis, "If saloon keepers and street car conductors are the men who are governing the United States, and lawyers and merchants are merely the ones being governed, then decidedly saloon keepers and street car conductors are the ones I want to know." And off he went to attend meetings of the Association in a great barnlike hall over a saloon in 59th Street. Joe Murray, a stockily built Irishman with a strong chin and twinkling eyes who had come to America steerage at the age of three, might not be so romatic as an old Norse Viking but he was a good fighter when it came to doing battle with the Political Ring and its "Big Boss" who had governed the Twenty-fifth District in their own interests for years. Young Roosevelt joined forces with Joe Murray, standing vehemently for whatever he deemed was right, and the first thing he knew he had defeated the Big Boss and his Ring and was elected a member of the New York State Assembly. There he was distinguishing himself for attacks on many corrupt practices that needed reforming when the death of his wife in 1883 sent him West to Chimney Butte.

The summer days following the coming of the women at Elkhorn were full of vigorous toil. Much of the time Roosevelt was away from the ranch on round-ups. He enjoyed enormously the rough but hearty comradeship of these gatherings which brought him in touch with the ranchmen and cowboys from hundreds of miles around. Whenever he arrived at the round-up he always reported at once to the Captain, who assigned him to some wagon-boss. He then deposited his bedding outside the ring in no one's way and ate his supper in silence, turning a deaf ear to certain gibing remarks that were certain to be made about "four eyes" for the cowboys regarded spectacles as the surest sign of a "dude". There were rough enough characters among those men, too, but Roosevelt's doctrine of "do your job and keep your mouth shut" as well as the absolute fearlessness with which he occasionally stood up to some "tough customer" who was attempting to make sport of him, usually kept him out of trouble.

Work on the round-up began at three in the morning with a yell from the cook and lasted till sundown or sometimes all the night through. In the morning the cowboys "rode the long circle" in couples, driving into the wagon-camp whatever animals were found in the hills. The afternoon was spent in the difficult and dangerous work of "cutting out" of the herd thus gathered the cattle belonging to the various brands. Representatives of each brand rode in succession into the midst of the herd, working the animal they were after gently to the edge, and then, with a sudden dash taking it off at a run. At night there was often guard duty about the restless herd. One evening a heavy storm broke over the camp. There was a terrific peal of thunder, and the lightning struck almost into the herd. Heads and tails high, off plunged the panic stricken cattle into the blackness, and for forty hours Roosevelt was in the saddle driving the scattered herd together again. After that the cow-punchers decided that the man with the four eyes "had the stuff in him" after all. And so, quietly "doing his job" day by day, accepting the discipline of the camp and the orders of the Captain of the Round-up, Roosevelt gradually won a place for himself in the rough world of the Bad Lands. He was not a crack rider or a fancy roper, just as it was true that he had never had a special gift in any line, but he was unflinchingly persistent in whatever he undertook and he put into all he did every ounce of energy and enthusiasm in him, so that he often outdid far more gifted men.

Winter passed and Spring came early that year at Elkhorn. About the middle of March a great ice jam came slowly drifting past the ranch, roaring and crunching, and piling the ice high on both banks, even grinding against the porch and the cottonwood trees and threatening to wash the house away. But the force of the freshet gradually carried the jam on. Then Bill Sewall dis-

covered that their one and only boat had been stolen from its moorings. Now there had recently been three suspicious characters seen in the neighborhood, thieves fleeing from justice, the leader of whom was a desperado named Finnegan, and the men did not doubt that they had stolen the boat. Roosevelt had been made a deputy sheriff and he conceived it to be his duty to start out after these thieves. The country was impassable on horses or foot, so Sewall and Dow built a flat-bottomed boat and in three days the men set out, with provisions for two weeks. The region through which they travelled was bleak and terrible. On either side beyond the piles of ice rose scarred buttes, weather-worn into the most fantastic shapes. It was zero weather, too, and there was an icy wind in their faces, but they found fire wood in plenty and prairie fowl and deer for every meal. Late on the third day, on rounding a bend, they suddenly saw their boat moored to the shore. Out of the bushes a little way back went curling the smoke of a camp-fire. The men leapt ashore and advanced cautiously through the underbush. Beside the fire, in the shelter of a cut-bank, they saw a solitary figure with a gun on the ground beside him. Hands up! Roosevelt and Dow rushed on the man, a half-witted German, who had been left to guard the camp while Finnegan and a half-breed Swede went hunting. The German made haste to obey. Sewall stood guard over him while Roosevelt and Dow crouched under the bank and waited for the others. At the end of an hour, they saw them leisurely coming through the grass. Roosevelt cried at once, "Hands up!" The Swede obeyed but Finnegan glared and hesitated. Then Roosevelt advanced on him covering him with his gun and repeating, "You thief, put up your hands." With an oath Finnegan dropped his rifle and obeyed.

That night the men from Elkhorn camped where they were, guarding their prisoners well, but the next day they found that their return passage had been barred by the ice jam which had floated down from Elkhorn. Day after day they waited hoping for a thaw. Their provisions ran short and there was no game to be found in that neighborhood. They were reduced for food to unleavened bread made with muddy water. So the days passed with utter tediousness and the thieves had to be watched every minute. At last Roosevelt, scouring the neighborhood, found an outlying cow-camp where he got a wiry, fractious little horse. On this he rode fifteen miles to a ranch where he secured supplies and a prairie schooner, hiring the ranchman to drive the wagon himself to the camp by the ice-bound river. Thus thoroughly provisioned again, Sewall and Dow waited with the boats while Roosevelt started out with the thieves and the prairie schooner for the nearest jail, a desolate ten days' journey across the prairie. Not for a moment did Roosevelt dare abate his watch on the prisoners so he made them get up into the wagon while he walked behind with his gun. Hour after hour he waded through ankle-deep mud, hungry, cold, fatigued, but now, as ever, determined to carry the matter through at any cost. The very last night they put up at the squalid hut of a frontier granger, but Roosevelt, weary as he was, dared not sleep. He crowded the prisoners into an upper bunk and sat against the cabin door till dawn with his gun across his knee. On the following evening he deposited the thieves in jail.

And so Theodore Roosevelt, living, talking, working, facing dangers and suffering hardships with Dow, Sewall, Merrifield,

Ferris and countless other stalwart citizens of the Bad Lands, came very close to the heart of the "plain American." But the day came at last when he found he must leave his beloved Elkhorn and return to New York. His ranch did not pay from the money standpoint. Moreover he was to marry again and life was calling him back to be a "doer of deeds" in another way.

Soon it was dishonesty and corruption he was fighting as a member of the United States Civil Service Commission. In 1895 he was doing the same as Police Commissioner of the City of New York, and when the tyranny and cruelty of Spain toward the little island of Cuba forced the United States to declare war on Spain, Roosevelt, then Assistant Secretary of the Navy under President McKinley, resigned his post at once and offered to recruit a regiment of mounted riflemen from among the skilled horsemen of the plains. Of this organization, the Rough Riders, Leonard Wood was Colonel and Theodore Roosevelt was Lieutenant Colonel. These were days for Roosevelt to remember his old friends of the Bad Lands and they came flocking to his standard. But the Rough Riders were not all cowboys; they were bronco-busters and Fifth Avenue aristocrats, western badmen and eastern college boys, a valiant, if motley crew. After the first battle of Las Guasimos in the Cuban jungle, Wood was advanced in command and Roosevelt was made Colonel of the Rough Riders. So it happened that at the decisive battle of San Juan Hill on the road to Santiago, it was Roosevelt, his face streaked with dirt and sweat, his trousers and boots caked with Cuban mud, a blue bandana handkerchief with white polka dots floating like a banner from his soiled campaign hat, whom the Rough Riders followed over crest after crest of the San Juan Hills, on, on to victory.

Overnight Roosevelt became a popular hero. He returned to the United States to be elected Governor of New York and two years later at the National Republican Convention a perfect stampede of western delegates forced him against his will to accept the

nomination for Vice President of the United States with William McKinley as President. Then came the day when McKinley was shot at Buffalo. The summons for Roosevelt reached him in the heart of the Adirondacks where he had just been climbing Mt. Marcy. In a light buckboard wagon, dashing along almost on one wheel over a well-nigh impassable road that had been cut into gorges only a day or two before by a cloudburst, Roosevelt went down through the night to the nearest railroad, with a heart awed by his great responsibility, to be President of the United States.

And now for a time he pursued no more buffalo and elk, but with the same dogged courage and persistence he had shown on the western plains, he pursued Big Business and Unjust Privilege, the Railroad Trust, the Beef Trust and all other big corporations who were defrauding the public. He settled a coal strike that threatened the welfare of all the country; he brought about peace between Russia and Japan in the days of the Russo-Japanese war; he put through the Panama Canal, and gradually he began to stand out everywhere in the world as the greatest and most typical American of all, one who knew no neutrality when Right or Wrong was the issue, but stood vigorously, aggressively if need be, for the Right, the very personification of that moral force in man which translates ideals into accomplished facts.

Important Works: Winning of the West Ranch Life and the Hunting Trail. The Rough Riders

ROSSETTI, CHRISTINA G. (English Poet, 1830–1894)

Important Works: The Goblin Market. Sing-Song (Beautiful Verses for Children)

RUSKIN, JOHN (English, 1819–1900)

THERE was once a small boy who deeply loved beauty. Even as a little fellow he was frequently taken to Europe in search of all that was lovely. By the time he was three years old he was already so fond of nature, that, when an artist who was painting his portrait asked him what he would like to have for a background behind him in the picture, he piped up at once and answered, "Blue hills."

When he grew to be a man, Ruskin began writing books about all the beautiful pictures he loved, eagerly aiming to show others how to see as much beauty in them as he did. Later, his interest in beauty advanced beyond pictures and he began writing books about how people could bring out more beauty in their lives by casting out ugly faults and more truly awaking to what is good. He had deeply at heart the welfare of boys and girls and while he was still a student at Oxford he set himself to please a little girl by writing the beautiful story of *The King of the Golden River*.

SANDBURG, CARL (American, 1878–)

A BOY driving a milk wagon in Illinois prairie blizzards, working in brickyards and potteries, swinging a pitchfork beside the threshing machine in Kansas wheatfields—that was Carl Sandburg. A youth working his way through college at Galesburg, Illinois, the town where he was born, washing dishes in Denver hotels, shoveling coal in Omaha, serving as a soldier in Porto Rico. A man working as newspaper correspondent in Sweden during the World War. Carl Sandburg is still a newspaper writer but he is also among the most important of modern American poets. His work is typically modern, written in free verse, and his subjects are those avoided by the older poets—the city, its beauty and ugliness. In short, forceful poems he flashes vivid impressions.

Important Works: Chicago Poems. Smoke and Steel.

SCOTT, SIR WALTER (Scotch, 1771–1832)

Under the ruins of an old castle in Scotland, a tiny boy once played on the soft green turf among the lambs and dogs. This was little Walter Scott who had been sent down from his home in Edinburgh to his grandfather's farm at Sandyknowe that he might live out of doors and grow strong, for the child had been lame from his babyhood. From his grandmother and aunt young Walter heard endless ballads of Scottish history and tales of the Border heroes. Before he could read he learned these ballads by heart and would shout them out lustily, much to the discomfort of the minister when he came to call for he could neither speak nor hear above such a clamor. But the boy was a most engaging little fellow and all his elders delighted to tell him stories.

Once his aunt took him to the theatre in London. The play was *As You Like It*, and it all seemed so real to Walter that when Orlando and Oliver fell to quarreling he cried out aloud in his shrill little voice, "But aren't they brothers?"

As soon as he was strong enough to go to school, he pursued his love of history and romance still further, ready to submit to any amount of dry work if he could only read more widely. Patiently he mastered both French and Italian in order to read in their own tongues the French and Italian romances. All his reading, however, never interfered with the boy's sports. In spite of his lameness he was always a leader in frolics and "high jinks." He wandered about the country, too, in search of ballads, and since he could not sketch the places he visited, he brought away branches of trees as souvenirs, eagerly planning to carve a set of chessmen—kings and queens from branches growing near palaces, bishops from those that had shaded an abbey.

When his education was finished Scott set up as a lawyer, but he soon began making splendid use of his ballad lore by writing *The Lay of the Last Minstrel, Marmion* and *The Lady of the Lake.* Presently he found himself famous as a poet. Then he bought himself a beautiful home at Abbotsford on the river Tweed, amid the gray hills and the heather of the border country that he loved so well. Scarcely had he done this when a certain swaggering little tailor, nick-named Rig-dum-funni-dos, whom he had placed at the head of a publishing house he had organized, involved him in immense business debts. To pay these off honorably Scott plunged at once into work and completed his first novel, *Waverley*. This he published without signing his name to it, and now in an incredibly short time he wrote novel after novel of that splendid Waverley series. Few even guessed that the hearty, hospitable country laird, keeping open house for all visitors at Abbotsford, living in fine old feudal fashion with baronial splendor and hospitality, was the author of these novels. Where did he ever find time to write them? Even the few who knew how early he rose to do his work, fancied he must have kept a goblin hidden away somewhere in attic or cellar to help him.

In 1825, after eleven years of brilliant and prosperous labor, just when he believed himself free from debts, he found he had been involved again through his publishing business to the amount of 130,000 pounds. To pay off this enormous debt, he toiled incessantly for seven years more. It was a heroic struggle but in the end his health broke down and he died at his beloved Abbotsford.

Important Works: Ivanhoe. Waverly. The Talisman. Count Robert of Paris. Guy Mannering.

SELVA, SALOMON DE LA (Nicaraguan, 1893–)

ALOMON DE LA SELVA was born in Leon, Nicaragua. His family is an old one, distinguished in politics and literature. Among them were Indian chiefs and Spanish conquistadores. He studied at home, in Europe and the United States and has also lectured on poetry at Columbia University. During the World War he fought with the British forces. He is considered the foremost poet of the day in Latin America, and upon his father's death was adopted as the nation's ward by decree of the Nicaraguan Congress.

*SHAKESPEARE, WILLIAM (English, 1564–1616)

Beyond Sir Hugh Clopton's noble old stone bridge that spans the Avon with fourteen splendid arches rise the quaint gables and cathedral spire of good old Stratford town. In the days of Queen Elizabeth the houses were ancient plaster buildings crossed with timber and each had at the sides or rear a gay little garden vivid with color. In one of the best of those houses on Henley Street, lived Master Will Shakespeare, a high spirited lad, with a fine, courtly bearing and pleasant hazel eyes. His father, John Shakespeare, was a well-to-do merchant, a trader in hides, leather-goods, wool, meats and goodness knows what else. He had once been High Bailiff or Mayor of the town. His mother, Mary Arden Shakespeare, was sweet and womanly, and the boy loved her dearly. Happy, indeed, was his merry little home circle.

Over in the old, old grammar school, whose jutting second story abutted on the street, Master Will and the other Stratford urchins learned their lessons, but it was a gay and joyous life, in spite of lessons, that they led in Stratford town. For Warwickshire in those days was divided into two well marked divisions by the river Avon. To the south lay the rich green pasture land of Feldon, stretching away to the blue line of the distant Cotswold hills, and dotted here and there by herds of cattle and flocks of snow-white sheep. Amid little clumps of protecting elms nestled

*Read *Master Skylark*, a story of Shakespeare's time, by John Bennett*

cozy homesteads, and past the well tilled fields flowed placid rivers, their limpid waters overhung by alders and silver willows. To the, north of the Avon, however—Ah! there was no cultivated land, but the wild, free forest of Arden, sweeping out over hill and dale for twenty miles, the delight of all boyish hearts. When school time was over, then for Will Shakespeare and the other Stratford boys it was Heigh and a Ho! for the Forest of Arden. O, the sweetness of those woodland haunts, the exhilaration and breadth and joy! The boys raced through leafy covert and sunny glade, past giant oaks and tangled thickets, now skipping from stone to stone across the brawling brooks, now cleaving the woodland stillness with their shrill young voices. Sometimes a dappled herd of deer would sweep away before them across an open lawn or twinkle through the leaves amid the shadowy bracken, while groups of timid rabbits fed here and there on the tender leaves. Will Shakespeare talked with every keeper and woodman in the forest and knew intimately all the ins and outs of that glorious sylvan life.

At times, too, young Will wandered through all the picturesque towns and little forest villages round about, past the old gray castles and abbeys that loomed within their parks shut off by palings from the wilderness of Arden. Some of these castles had been abandoned and dismantled during the Wars of the Roses. Silent now as the surrounding forest they stood, half ruined, and haunted with shadowy memories of lords and ladies and all the stately revelry that had once held sway within their walls. It was a country full of interest, full of history, full of story, full of stirring border legends of the days when the English stood sturdily against the insurgents of Wales. Every hill and stream, every grim old abbey and castle had its heroic tale of long ago.

On market days and fair days there was great

excitement in the town itself for Master Will Shakespeare, for Stratford was the center of a great grazing and agricultural district. On a bright summer's day Will would rise with the sun and make off from Henley Street to watch the droves of slow oxen come crowding in over Clopton Bridge, and the herds of Herefordshire cows, lowing anxiously after their skittish young calves. Then he would follow the cattle to Rother Market, where the cattle dealers gathered about Market Cross, and observe the humors of the ploughman and drovers, scarcely less stolid and deliberate of movement and speech than their oxen. Over by the High Cross, a solid stone building with steps below and open arches above, the traders in corn and country produce held market. A gay and lively scene was Stratford on market day.

Not far from Stratford lay the little forest village of Snitterfield, where Will's grandfather and Uncle Henry Shakespeare had farms. Every boundary tree and stone, every pond and sheep-pool, every barn and cattleshed on the way to his Uncle Henry's farm Will knew by heart, for he dearly loved the place and spent many a happy day there. At Snitterfield Will trotted around after his uncle, poking into all the byres and barns and poultry yards, and the man was charmed at the boy's eager interest. Now and again from a safe nook on the bushy margin of a pool, he enjoyed the fun and excitement of the sheep washing, or watched the mysteries of the sheep shearing. Then he would remain to the shearing feast and see the young maid who was chosen Queen of the Festival receive her rustic guests and distribute among them her gifts of flowers. Indeed, young Will Shakespeare's youth was passed amid the labors and pastimes, the recurring festivals and varying round of a rural community. Each incident of the year, seedtime and harvest, summer and winter, brought its own group of picturesque merry-makings in those forest farms and villages.

The chief holiday of all was May-day with its masques and morris-dances, its hobby horses making continuous merriment, and its maypoles decked with gay-colored streamers and fragrant garlands. What a day it was! In the streets of Stratford leafy screens and arches were erected, and everywhere were garlands of flowers, brought in from the forest at dawn by rejoicing youths and maidens. A spontaneous outburst of joy, a gladsome welcome to the re-awakening life and vernal freshness of the Spring! Sometimes, too, there were acted out on May-day the exploits of Robin Hood and Maid Marian, but it was usually at Whitsuntide, the next important holiday after May-day, that those exhibitions nearest to play-acting were given. What queer old pageants they were, following the procession of trade-guilds and the usual holiday sports.

The very oldest form of play that the people loved in England was the miracle or mystery play, presenting usually some tale from the Bible. At first, long years before Shakespeare's time, these plays had been given in the churches by the clergy, then, gradually they had moved out to the church yard and the actors had changed from the clergy to citizens, members of the various trade guilds. Later still they were given on a cart, called the pageant cart, which was moved about from place to place, giving a performance wherever it stopped. They would play the story of Noah's flood, or Adam and Eve, or the Destruction of Jerusalem, or some such subject. The lower part of the cart was draped with cloth which hid the wheels, and behind this screen the actors dressed and kept their machinery. In the Destruction of Jerusalem, for example, it was necessary to keep there a quantity of starch to make a storm, some barrels which were rolled around to produce thunder, and a windlass to make an earthquake. The action of the play took place on the flat part of the cart, but sometimes the actors stepped down into the street, and the lower part of the cart had to be used whenever they wanted to present such a scene as the grim and gaping jaws of Hell, whence issued devils, dressed in black and yellow to represent flames. Herod and Pilate, Cain and Judas, and certain turbaned Turks and infidels as well as

the Devil were favorite characters of these mysteries. The Devil wore black leather covered with hair and had a grotesque painted head, and most of the actors either wore masks or had their faces much painted. Vice was a constant attendant on the Devil, but he gradually changed into a mere buffoon or clown. In time morality plays became even more popular than the mysteries. In the moralities, all manner of Vices and all manner of Virtues were portrayed as persons who did battle with each other in order to gain possession of man's soul. It was some such performances as these that Will Shakespeare used to see as a boy, though in his day it was rather customary to draw the pageant cart up in the courtyard of some inn. The common people would then crowd around it, standing, while the richer ones paid a large fee to have seats in the balconies or windows of the inn that overlooked the courtyard.

Coventry, a town near Stratford, was one of the chief centers for the production of miracle plays and Shakespeare must have gone over there sometimes to see them. Moreover, the various trade guilds, plasterers, tanners, armourers, hosiers, etc. who presented the plays were in the habit of visiting neighboring cities and doubtless performed in Stratford. When Will was only five years old, his father, then Mayor of Stratford, had especially invited the stage players to Stratford and started a series of performances in the Guild Hall. Later, the best companies in the kingdom used to come to Stratford, including the Earl of Leicester's Company from London. So young Master Will had plenty of opportunity to study the making and presenting of plays, to acquire a deep love for the theatre and perhaps sometimes even to act himself and make friends with the players.

But now when Will was still little more than a boy, his father began to have business failures and his affairs to go down, down, down in the world, so the lad was taken from school and put to work, to help out in his father's business. John Shakespeare had been imprudently extravagant in his prosperity and now he simply lost his grip and let himself sink down under misfortune, shunning society and refusing to go to church or any public meeting. Sweet Mary Shakespeare, however, bore up nobly against their troubles, her spirit as calm and serene in the dark days as it had been in the bright. How the boy loved and admired his mother. She was to remain in his heart all his days as the very embodiment of every womanly virtue. Will sympathized with his parents in their troubles and was willing to do any kind of work to help them. Moreover, those very troubles awakened his independence and taught him to be scrupulously honorable in his own business dealings with others, a trait which he never forgot. An open, frank, generous young fellow was Will Shakespeare in those days, innately courteous and wholly lovable.

When Will was only eighteen, he was often to be seen making off across the fields, pied with daisies, to the little hamlet of Shottery, which lay half concealed by aged elms, its cozy homesteads nestling amid blossoming fruit-trees and brilliant gardens. Here in a lovely old cottage, with a quaint thatched roof, lived Anne Hathaway, the daughter of a friend of Will's father, a maid whom he had known all his life. In the garden and through the primrose lanes the two lingered often together and soon there was news of their wedding. Boy that he was, Will was only nineteen when his first daughter, Suzanne, was born. Now what was there to do? He had a family on his hands to support and his father's business grew every day worse and worse. Two years later twins were born to him, a boy and a girl, Hamnet and Judith, and then an event occurred which made the young man decide that the only thing for him to do was to be off to London and seek there his fortunes as a player, as doubtless he had long desired to do. He was off hunting one day with some young comrades when they pursued a fine deer into Fullbroke Park, or perhaps across the shallow ford of the river to Charlecote Park, the property of a sour and gloomy old Puritan, Sir Thomas Lucy, a man of aristocratic pride and narrowness who hated all youthful frolics and merriment. Just as they had killed the buck the youths fell in with one of Sir Thomas's keepers, who insisted violently that they had no right to hunt where they were and accused them of deer-stealing. Master Will defended himself right spiritedly against the charge and so aroused the wrath of Sir Thomas that he complained to the Stratford authorities. They, fearing to offend so rich and powerful a man, doubtless let it be known to Will that he would better leave town for a time. Accordingly, behold young Will, bidding his wife and babes farewell and off for London town.

It was about 1585 or 1587 when Will Shakespeare arrived in London. In those days players were just beginning to be recognized as respectable folk. Certain writers of education, such as

Greene and Peele and Marlowe, had been among the first to think the writing of plays a vocation worthy of their dignity, and were turning out plays vastly more like modern dramas than the old morality and miracle plays. Ten years before, Queen Elizabeth had given the Earl of Leicester's players the first legal permit to act in certain places in London, and James Burbage, the leader of these players had built *The Theatre* at Shoreditch, just outside the boundaries of London, for mayor and common council still frowned on plays within the city. In building his theatre, Burbage took his plan from the old courtyards of the inns where it had been customary to draw up the pageant carts. The square yard where poorer people stood, became the pit of the theatre, the pageant cart the stage, and the windows whence the wealthier class had looked on, the gallery or boxes. The stage and galleries were the only part of the building covered, which was none too comfortable for people in the pit if a sudden storm came pelting down. But rude as this theatre was, to Burbage belongs the honor of first establishing theatres as a part of city life and removing from actors the stigma of being strolling players.

Here at *The Theatre* Master Will first found occupation by holding the horses of the gallants who attended, and organizing a corps of boys to help him. But he soon advanced from that work to acting within the theatre, then to writing over faulty old plays, and at last to writing those splendid plays of his own. In a very short time he had surpassed all the dramatists of his day, Greene and Peele and Marlowe and all, and held the foremost place in the hearts of the play-going public. Yet with all his success he kept his head marvelously well, avoiding all the wild dissipations of his fellow-dramatists, though he loved life and mirth as well as any and hadn't a trace of harshness or severity in his character. He worked hard, studying at French and Italian in his spare time, saving money for his family and making yearly visits to Stratford.

He was first a member of the Earl of Leicester's players which

later became the Lord Chamberlain's Company and the favorite company of the Queen. All the players in London in those days save for certain bands of children players were divided into two companies, the Lord Admiral's and the Lord Chamberlain's. The theatres where Shakespeare's plays were given were *The Globe*, erected outside the city, and *Blackfriar's*, which was practically in the city. The actors played at *The Globe* in summer and at *Blackfriar's* in the winter. *Blackfriar's* was completely roofed in and lit by torchlight so performances could be given there in the evening, but at *The Globe* the pit was uncovered and performances were only given by day. The common people had a merry time standing in the pit, munching apples and nuts, while the aristocrats had their own boxes wherein the ladies occupied the seats with the gentlemen reclining at their feet. If they chose, they played cards during the performance and there were always pages ready to attend upon them. Whoever paid extra could sit upon the stage itself. There was no scenery on that stage and a simple printed placard announced the name of the place where the scene was supposed to be laid. Women's parts were taken by men. It was not until long after Shakespeare's time that women appeared on the stage. The hoisting of a flag and blowing of a trumpet bade all be still to hear the play.

What an age of awakened national life and stirring spirit was that of Elizabeth, when the minds of men had burst the bonds of the Dark Ages and were eagerly inquiring and adventuring everywhere. Along the river side and in noble houses on the Strand were the hardy mariners and adventurous sea captains, Drake, Hawkins and Frobisher, who had driven their dauntless keels fearlessly into the unknown seas of the new world, in order to push back the limits of man's knowledge. The greater number of eager and excited listeners who crowded the rude theatres from floor to roof had shared the adventurous exploits of the age and all felt the keenest interest in life and action. So the drama of the day became the mirror in which all these active forces were reflected. And beside the Americas there was another new world which men were most anxious to explore in that age of awakened inquiry, the world of human nature, heretofore left so little questioned and understood. All the traits and impulses of that nature, good and bad, its high hopes and aspirations, its fears and sorrows, its bigness and its littleness,—there was need of a chart to point them all out. Into that unknown sea sailed the intrepid mariner Shakespeare and charted it in his mighty dramas as none other has ever done, the great Columbus of the newly discovered world of man's heart and mind and spirit.

For twenty years he worked actively in London, twenty long years, but at last a great wave of home-yearning called him back to the primrose lanes of Stratford. He had already bought a fine house there for his family and here he settled down, to spend his remaining years in peace and quiet, honored and loved by all. No other man ever knew the hearts of men and women as Shakespeare did. He still remains the greatest dramatist of all ages and all races who wrote "not for an age but for all time".

Read Tales from Shakespeare by Charles and Mary Lamb

SHELLEY, PERCY BYSSHE (English, 1792–1822)

PERCY BYSSHE SHELLEY was the son of a stubborn, old, English baronet, Sir Timothy Shelley, who was tyrannical and harsh in his own home and yet observed ceremoniously all the outward forms of religion. The boy had a beautiful, gifted mother, but his father's character made him early learn to hate oppression and a religion that was all show and no spirit. At school he was a shy boy, persecuted and made fun of by his fellows, and this still further strengthened his hatred of oppression. At seventeen he was expelled from Oxford for writing a pamphlet concerning religion. His father then angrily forbade him the house and he made the sad mistake of marrying a young girl of sixteen, Harriet Westbrook, a school friend of his sister's, who appealed to his sense of chivalry and made him believe that she was ill-used at home. Young Shelley had a perfect passion for justice and freedom, downright sincerity and truth, and he longed to establish an ideal state of love and brotherhood. At nineteen the fiery youth set off to redress the wrongs of Ireland. A little later, he wrote several revolutionary pamphlets in England which he sent to sea in bottles and boxes for winds and waves to circulate. These made it necessary for him to flee for a time into Wales. When he was twenty one, he separated from his young wife and went to France and Italy where he spent the rest of his life with Mary Godwin Shelley, his second wife. He was a great friend of Byron and Keats and one of England's foremost poets. At thirty he was drowned while sailing on the Mediterranean.

SHEPARD, ODELL (American poet and literary critic, 1884–)

SOUTHEY, ROBERT (English, 1774–1843)

Poet of the Lake District. Friend of Wordsworth and Coleridge.

SPENSER, EDMUND (English, 1552–1599)

One of the supremely great poets of Queen Elizabeth's period.

SPYRI, JOHANNA (Swiss writer of children's stories, 1829–)

Cornelli *Heidi.* *Moni, the Goat Boy.* *Rico and Wiseli.*

STEDMAN, EDMUND CLARENCE (American critic, 1833–1908)

STEVENSON, ROBERT LOUIS (Scotch, 1850–1894)

ROBERT LOUIS STEVENSON was born in Edinburgh. He was the son of a noted engineer who had the interesting task of planning and building great light-houses that flashed out their signal lights all along the Scottish coast. The boy's father intended him likewise for an engineer, but Robert was scarcely strong enough for such a life, so he studied to be a lawyer. When he was a young man he once went off with his canoe to paddle through the canals and rivers, the quaint, trim villages and pleasant fields of Belgium and France. He followed this with a walking trip through the rich beauties of Southern France, having as his only companion a particularly stubborn donkey. When he returned to England he wrote so delightfully of these journeys, *An Inland Voyage*, and *Travels With A Donkey*, that his friends began to urge him to give up other work and do nothing but write.

A year or so later, Stevenson heard that the young lady whom he was to marry, a Mrs. Osbourne, was ill in California, so he set out to join her. Travel was expensive and he had little money, so what did he do but go as a steerage passenger on the boat among all the hodge-podge of immigrants—queer characters, jabbering the strange tongues of half the countries of Europe. Then he crossed the American continent on an immigrant train. In San Francisco he married Mrs. Osbourne and after some months in a desolate mining camp, he returned with her and his little stepson to Scotland. Stevenson had never been strong or well, though he was the cheeriest man imaginable and never let ill health keep him from work. In the years following his marriage he wandered about with his family into all sorts of curious places, seeking a spot where he could live more comfortably. At last he

settled down on one of the Samoan Islands, a tropical paradise amid the soft blue waters of the South Seas. Here he had a beautiful place called Vailima at the foot of a lofty mountain. How truly he enjoyed making acquaintance with the simple, hospitable, brown-skinned natives. He acquired great influence in their affairs and used to sit in state at their councils.

In spite of his physical weakness, Stevenson was ever at work, writing, writing, and his heart was so full of keen boyish love of adventure that he left boys and girls such stories as no man has ever surpassed. In 1894 he died at Vailima as courageously and cheerily as he had lived, and his body was borne by sixty natives up Mt. Vaea to rest in a beautiful spot above his home.

Treasure Island. Kidnapped. The Master of Ballantrae. Child's Garden of Verse.

STOCKTON, FRANCIS R. (American novelist, 1834–1902)

Important Works: The Bee Man of Orn. Fanciful Tales. The Adventures of Captain Horn.

STOWE, HARRIET BEECHER (American, 1811–1896)

Mrs. Stowe is best known as the author of *Uncle Tom's Cabin.*

SWINBURNE, ALGERNON C. (English poet, 1837–1909)

TAGORE, RABINDRANATH (East Indian, 1861–)

TAGORE was born in Calcutta. Very early he lost his mother, and his regret colors all his poems of mother and child love. He was a lonely little fellow for his father was often away from home. Nature, the clouds in the sky, the flowers, the leaves, were his beloved companions. A harsh master made his school days very unhappy, so he ran away. Then his father gave him private tutors and took him to the Himalayas where he studied and began to write songs and stories. At twenty-three he married and was sent to manage his father's estates on the Ganges. He went unwillingly at first, but soon he realized with deep satisfaction the joy of coming so closely in touch with his people. Here he wrote many of his best plays. When he was forty he lost his wife, his daughter and his young son. In his sorrow and restlessness he started a boy's school which he aimed to make a model place where boys could be educated with all the freedom and self government possible. Tagore is one of the greatest East Indian thinkers.

TAYLOR, BAYARD (American writer and traveler, 1825–'78)

TAYLOR, JANE (English children's poet, 1783–1824)

TENNYSON, ALFRED, LORD (English, 1809–1892)

Alfred Tennyson's father was the rector of Somersby and the boy lived in a quiet, pleasant home where there was plenty of time for reading and reflection. He was always the story-teller for his brothers and sisters, and his favorite game was to write endless romances which he slipped under the dishes at table to be read when the business of eating was over. When he was only eighteen he and his brother Charles published a volume of verse called, *Poems by Two Brothers.* From then on, Alfred slowly rose, struggling often against poverty, to be Poet Laureate and the best loved poet in England.

Idylls of the King. The Princess. Tennyson for the Young by Ainger.

THACKERAY, WILLIAM MAKEPEACE (English, 1811–1863)

Thackeray was born in Calcutta. His father died when he was a tiny boy and his mother married again. His step-father was a kindly gentleman very like the dear old Colonel Newcome in one of Thackeray's stories. While his mother and stepfather stayed in India, William was sent to England to be educated. He was not happy at school, for the boys were rough while he was gentle, and he was not overly clever at lessons or games. As a young man, Thackeray studied drawing in Paris, but he could not support himself by drawing, so he began to write. *The Book of Snobs*, published in *Punch*, brought him great success. Unfortunately Thackeray's young wife had become insane and his two little daughters were henceforth his constant companions. In his novels, which are accurate pictures of the life of his time, he holds up to sharp ridicule the snobbery he detested. He has written one book for children, the deliciously funny *Rose and the Ring*.

THAXTER, CELIA (American, 1836–1894)

Born in Portsmouth, N. H. Lived at the Isles of Shoals.

THOMPSON SETON, ERNEST (English, 1860–)

A well known writer of true animal stories. He was born in England but lived in Canada and on the western plains in boyhood.

Wild Animals I Have Known. Biography of a Grizzly. Lives of the Hunted.

THORNE-THOMSEN, GUDRUN (Contemporary)

One of the most satisfactory editors of Norse Tales for children.

Important Works: East 'O the Sun and West 'O the Moon. The Birch and the Star.

TOLSTOY, LYOF N. (Russian, 1828–1910)

At Yasnaya Polyana, which means "bright glade", lived young Lyof Tolstoy, a sensitive, plain-appearing little fellow of strong affections who loved games, and horses, and dogs, and country life. Bright Glade was a pretty place, a large wooden house surrounded by woods and avenues of lime trees, with a river and four lakes on the estate. Lyof's father and mother died when he was small and he was brought up by his aunt, Tatiana, whom he

loved very dearly. She used to welcome all sorts of queer pilgrims to Bright Glade, beggars and monks and poor despised wanderers, so the boy's life was always simple and unworldly.

One day Lyof's brother, Nicholas, invented a game called "ant brothers." He bade Lyof and the other two brothers crawl under two armchairs, hide themselves from view with handkerchiefs and boxes, and cling lovingly together in the dark. Then he told them that he possessed a secret, which, when it was known, would make all men happy. There would be no more disease, no trouble, and no one would be angry with anyone else. All would love one another and become "ant brothers." This secret he said he had written on a green stick and buried by the road at the edge of a certain ravine. The boys played the game often, but the great secret was never revealed to them. Nevertheless, that secret, the way for men to cease from suffering, to leave off quarreling and be always happy, was what Lyof sought all his life.

At Bright Glade Tolstoy lived with a wife and thirteen jolly children, writing books and joining in all the family sports. But more and more he came to hate the idle, frivolous, useless life of the rich, the injustice of governments and society which gave so much to the rich and so little to the poor, the jealousies and selfishness that made war among men, and finally he gave up everything else that he might devote himself to making happier lives for the poor serfs who labored on his estates. He tried to get back to the pure Christianity that Jesus taught, to lead a life of simplicity and work, of love and brotherhood. And so he lived among his peasants, sharing the hardest manual labor and dressing just as they did, a smock in summer, a sheepskin coat and cap in winter. The tyrannical Russian government of those days frowned darkly on his views, but more and more men looked to him as a great leader, thinker and teacher. When he was over seventy Tolstoy wrote, "The ideal of 'ant brothers', lovingly clinging to one another, though not under two arm chairs curtained by handkerchiefs, but of all mankind under the wide dome of heaven, has remained the same for me. As I then believed that there existed a little green stick whereon was written the message that could destroy all evil in men and give them universal welfare, so I now believe that such truth exists and will be revealed to men and will give them all it promises."

Important works: Gospel Stories. Twenty Three Tales. In Pursuit of Happiness.

TOPELIUS, ZACHARIAS (Finnish poet and novelist, 1818–'98)

TROWBRIDGE, JOHN TOWNSEND (Am. novelist, 1827–1916)

VAN DYKE, HENRY (American clergyman and writer, 1852–)

Important Works: The First Christmas Tree. The Blue Flower. The Story of the Other Wise Man.

WARNER, CHARLES DUDLEY (American editor, 1829–1900)

WATTS, ISAAC (English hymn writer and preacher, 1674–1748)

WHITE, STEWARD EDWARD (American novelist, 1873–)

Adventures of Bobby Orde. The Magic Forest. Gold (California in 1849.)

WHITTIER, JOHN GREENLEAF (American poet, 1807–1892)

Whittier was born in Haverhill, Mass., of a hard-working Quaker family. As a small boy he wrote poetry which he hid from everyone but his older sister. One day the postman tossed him a newspaper and what should he see but one of his own verses in print. His sister had sent it in, and from now on he contributed regularly to the paper. Soon the editor, William Lloyd Garrison, grew interested in him, sought him out, and urged him to educate himself. So the boy earned his tuition at Haverhill Academy by making slippers at eight cents apiece. He grew up to be the great poet of the anti-Slavery movement. His office was burned and he was mobbed for his views, but he continued to write poems full of rugged strength and deep religious feeling.

WILDE, OSCAR (English dramatist and novelist, 1856–1900)

Important Works: The Happy Prince and Other Stories.

WILSON, WOODROW (American, 1856–)

Woodrow Wilson was born in Virginia, brought up and educated in Georgia and South Carolina. As President of Princeton University, as Governor of New Jersey and as President of the United States, (1912-1920) he instituted great reforms always along the lines of more truly democratic ideals. During the World War it was he who first made plain to the world that what the allies were really fighting to protect and uphold was the principle of democratic government. It was also he who sought to work toward a lasting foundation for peace by urging persistently on the world the League of Nations.

WORDSWORTH, WILLIAM (English poet, 1770–1850)

Young William Wordsworth loved to ramble high up into the hills near his home, beside the lakes and sounding cataracts, until all Nature came to life, and flowers and mists and winds found voice and spoke to him. They told him he was one with all that overflowing Soul that lives throughout the universe, and in his joy it seemed to him that he "saw blessings spread around him like a sea." So the boy grew up pure in heart and content with modest pleasures. All his life long he loved to tramp and often his sister Dorothy was his comrade. With all his worldly goods done up in a handkerchief, he tramped through France in the early days of the French Revolution; he walked through England, Scotland, Wales and many parts of Europe. At last he settled down with Dorothy at Grasmere in the beautiful Lake Country, to seek in solitude a deeper understanding of the universe and to express in poetry all the songs that Nature sang to his inmost heart. Here, likewise, he married and found a warm friend in the poet, Coleridge, who lived near by. But while Coleridge aimed to make the weird and supernatural seem real in his poetry, Wordsworth aimed with deep simplicity to write of the commonplace, and to find in the humblest lives nobility and strength.

YONGE, CHARLOTTE (English novelist, 1823–1901)

ZANGWILL, ISRAEL (A great Jewish writer of England, 1864–)

THE INTERESTING HISTORY OF OLD MOTHER GOOSE

The most remarkable dame in all history who was born gray-headed and yet never grows old, who perennially keeps her charm, who is ever, forever, calling out the spirit of childhood in the human heart to go gamboling with her over the green, turning somersaults, kicking up its heels, and yet learning, too, at her knee from her quaint store of sage and precious nonsense, is that beloved old creature, Old Mother Goose. Who she was, and how she was, and why she was, who knows? Her personality remains enshrouded in the most delightful mystery. But for myself I believe she has dwelt forever in the human heart. Her rhymes and jingles are nothing more nor less than the spontaneous bubblings of the eternal spirit of childhood, that delicious, joyous, nonsensical wisdom which is foolishness only to men.

The rhymes and jingles of Old Mother Goose are a gradual growth like the old folk tales, composed at no one time by no one individual, but springing up all down through the ages, who knows how?—naturally, spontaneously, joyously, like the droll little Jack-in-the-Pulpits and Dutchmen's-Breeches of the woodland. They need no other claim to a reason for being than the pure joy of expressing that bubbling spirit (albeit sometimes by means of well nigh meaningless words) and the everlasting delight of man in rhyme and rhythm and musical arrangement of sounds. What other excuse for existence, save its beautiful arrangement of s's, is needed by that immortal line—"Sing a Song of Sixpence!"—

There have been many interesting theories as to the origin of the name Mother Goose. But the one most stoutly maintained was advanced in the quaint little volume published at Boston in the year 1833 by the firm of Munroe and Frances, under the title, "The Only True Mother Goose, without addition or abridgment, embracing also a reliable Life of the Goose Family never before published."

According to this story a certain Thomas Fleet, born in England, and brought up in a printing office in the city of Bristol, came to Boston in the year 1712, when that city was little more than an over-grown village, with its narrow, crooked streets still bespeaking the cow-paths from which they sprang. Here Thomas Fleet established a printing office in that street of the delectable name, Pudding Lane, where he published small books, pamphlets and such matter as came to his hands. It was not long before he became acquainted with a well-to-do family of the name of Goose, and he grew exceedingly fond of the pretty young daughter, Elizabeth Goose. Under the date June 8, 1715, there appears in the record of marriages still preserved in the historic old town hall of Boston, an entry recording the wedding by the famous Reverend Cotton Mather, of Thomas Fleet, "now residing in Pudding Lane of this city, to Elizabeth Goose."

The happy couple took up their residence in the same quaint little house with the small paned windows where the printing office was situated in Pudding Lane, and Elizabeth's mother, Old Mother Goose, went to live with them. Here various children were born to the Fleets, and Old Mother Goose, being a most devoted grandmother, was so over-joyed that she spent the greater part of her time in the nursery, pouring out to the little ones the songs and ditties which she had learned in her childhood.

The industrious father Fleet, having these ditties constantly dinned into his ears, shrewdly conceived the idea of turning the discomfort thus caused him to some good account by collecting the songs and publishing them. This he did under the title, *Songs for the Nursery or Mother Goose's Melodies*, and he sold the same from the Pudding Lane shop for the price of two coppers apiece. The story further goes on to relate how a goose with a very long neck and a wide open mouth flew across the title page of the book; and Munroe and Frances solemnly announced that they had merely reprinted these wonderful original verses.

This interesting, picturesque, and delightful tale may or may not be true. Certainly the grave of Old Mother Goose remains to this very day carefully marked in one of Boston's old churchyards, where it is visited by many devoted pilgrims each year, but unfortunately, no scrap of the original book has ever been found to corroborate the claim of Messrs. Munroe and Frances. Moreover, whether the tale be true or not, it still in no way explains the origin of the name Mother Goose. For in the very childhood of Thomas Fleet, more than twenty years before his supposed publication of Mother Goose's Melodies, there appeared in France a little prose collection of the best known fairy tales, Cinderella, Little Red Riding Hood, Toads and Diamonds, Bluebeard, Sleeping Beauty, etc. These were written by a most distinguished French writer, Charles Perrault, were published in Paris in the year 1697, and were called *Contes de ma Mere, l'Oye*, or, *Tales of My Mother, the Goose*. On the frontispiece of his book is an old woman spinning and telling tales to a man, a girl, a boy and a cat. It is not even known whether Perrault originated the name Mother Goose, for it is said, that long before his time even, the goose had been given the reputation of story telling. Instead of saying of stories the origin of which they did not care to disclose, "A little bird told me!" people used to say, "Oh, a goose told me!" And so, after all, perhaps even the name Mother Goose belongs to the people and not to any one individual.

These tales of Perrault's, however, were all in prose while it is through her rhymes and jingles that Mother Goose has won her best-deserved fame. The first known collection of rhymes under her name was published in London about 1765, having been gathered together by John Newbery, the famous publisher of St. Paul's Churchyard, and the first publisher in the world to give special attention to children's books. It was he who published *Little Goody Two-shoes*, the story generally attributed to the great and lovable Irish author, Oliver Goldsmith, the prime friend of children, and undoubtedly it was Goldsmith who edited the Mother Goose Melodies for Newbery. In Welsh's *Life of Goldsmith* we are told that Goldsmith taught a certain little maid "Jack and Jill by two bits of paper on his fingers," and that after the successful production of his play *The Good-natured Man*, Mr. Goldsmith was so overjoyed that he sang lustily for his friends his favorite song, "about an old woman tossed in a blanket seventeen times as high as the moon."

In 1785 Newbery's edition of Mother Goose was reprinted in Worcester, Massachusetts, by Isaiah Thomas, who had married one of the grand-daughters of Thomas Fleet, and a great-grand daughter of old Dame Goose. A very beautiful copy of this book is to be found in the Boston Library and, since the story of Thomas Fleet's edition cannot be proved, John Newbery must be accepted as the first publisher, and Isaiah Thomas as the first American publisher, of our best beloved nursery classic.

Some twenty years after the Thomas edition, another collection of nursery rhymes appeared, called Gammer Gurton's Garland, which contained all of the Mother Goose Melodies and a great many more besides, but much of this material was taken from old jest books, and was worthless and coarse, and Gammer Gurton's Garland never attained the popularity of Mother Goose.

In 1842, James Halliwell, a man of fine scholarship, made a careful study of the nursery rhymes of England, collected principally from oral tradition. He writes that these nonsense scraps "have come down in England to us in such numbers that in the short space of three years the author has collected considerably more than a thousand." Besides Halliwell, many other men of the highest literary ability have edited Mother Goose.

It is intensely interesting to know how very old some of our best known rhymes are. In the preface to the Newbery edition, the writer, probably Oliver Goldsmith, says, "The custom of singing these songs and lullabies to children is of very great antiquity. It is even as old as the time of the ancient Druids. Charactacus, King of the Britons, was rocked in his cradle in the Isle of Mona, now called Anglesea, and tuned to sleep by some of these soporiferous sonnets," Old King Cole was certainly an ancient Celtic king of about the third century A. D., an original Briton, who lived even before the Angles and Saxons had come to conquer England. Dim and far away seem those days in the dawn of English history, when the Druids still held sway with the dark mysteries of their religion in the dusky oak forests of England, but the whole flashes suddenly into light and life when we realize that those were the very days when

Old King Cole
Was a merry old soul
And a merry old soul was he;
Old King Cole
He sat in his hole,
And called for his fiddlers three.
And every fiddler, he had a fine fiddle,
And a very fine fiddle had he,
"Tweedledee, tweedledee," said the fiddlers three.

Little Jack Horner, too, is probably early Celtic and was originally a long poem, containing the *Pleasant History of all Jack Horner's Witty Pranks*, of which the sticking of his thumb in the Christmas pie formed only an insignificant part.

Mother, May I Go Out to Swim? is fourteen hundred years old and comes from a jest book of the sixth century. Only to think that at the same time when minstrels were singing with wondrous dignity to courtly listeners in the great halls of the castles, the sonorous and heroic lines of the Beowulf, children in the nursery were snickering and giggling, just as we do today, over the ridiculous jingle,

Mother, may I go out to swim?
Yes, my darling daughter,
Hang your clothes on a hickory limb,
But don't go near the water!

And for every one man of this present time who knows the classic Beowulf, there are at least five hundred who know the jingle!

I Had a Little Husband No Bigger Than My Thumb is probably a part of Tom Thumb's History and is supposed to have originated in the tenth century from a little Danish work treating of "Swain Tomling, a man no bigger than a thumb, who would be married to a woman three ells and three quarters long."

Humpty Dumpty dates back to the days of King John in the thirteenth century. When that tyrannical gentleman was quarreling with his barons and they were forcing him to grant them the Great Charter of England, Humpty Dumpty had already begun his immortal escapade of falling off the wall, and if one were to inquire which had won the more enduring fame by his exploits, the answer would necessarily be, that granting the foundation for all the liberties of England, could never place King John in the same rank with that prime entertainer of infancy, who will apparently be performing his antics unto all generations.

The rhyme of the old woman who was tossed up in a blanket was old in the days of Henry V, in the early fifteenth century.

When that strong-handed monarch set out with a mere handful of men to conquer France, the faction opposed to him in his own country, used to sing the rhyme to ridicule him and show the folly and impossibility of his undertaking, representing the King as an old woman engaged in a pursuit the most absurd and extravagant possible. But when King Henry routed the whole French army at Agincourt, taking their king and the flower of their nobility prisoners, and made himself master of France in spite of his mere handful of men, the very people who had ridiculed him began to change their minds and think no task too difficult for him. They therefore cancelled the former sonnet and sang this one:

So vast is the prowess of Harry the Great,
He'll pluck a hair from the pale faced moon;
Or a lion familiarly take by the tooth,
And lead him about as you lead a baboon.
All princes and potentates under the sun,
Through fear into corners and holes away run;
While no danger nor dread his swift progress retards,
For he deals with kingdoms as we do our cards!

The Queen whom Pussy Cat, Pussy Cat, made the famous expedition to London to see, appears to have been Queen Elizabeth, though why Pussy Cat, Pussy Cat reported nothing more interesting at court than frightening a little mouse under a chair, when she might have held forth on the subject of Queen Elizabeth in all the glory of her satins and jewels, and stomachers, and puffs, and ruffs, and coifs, remains a secret known only to Pussy.

Simple Simon comes also from a chap-book of the Elizabethan era. These chap-books were small volumes carried about from place to place for sale by itinerant merchants or chap-men. It was from such books that a great number of the old rhymes came.

Sing a Song of Sixpence was well known in Shakespeare's time.

The unfortunate Hector Protector who was dressed all in green and met with such disfavor at the hands of the King as well as the Queen, was that doughty old Puritan, Oliver Cromwell, Lord High Protector of England, familiarly called Old Noll, who ousted Charles I from his throne and could scarcely be expected, henceforth, to be any too graciously dealt with by kings and queens.

From all this account which might be lengthened still further, it appears that Old Mother Goose is no mere modern upstart, but belongs to the pedigreed aristocracy of literature and must be treated with becoming consideration and respect. Nevertheless, it cannot be denied that, beside all the precious pearls of pure and joyous nonsense which Mother Goose has given us, she has perpetrated certain unworthy pranks in the form of coarse and vulgar rhymes, for which she needs to be given some broth without any bread, whipped very soundly and sent off to bed. In other words, from the very nature of the old jest books from which much of Mother Goose was taken, too many collections contain objectionable rhymes, and the need for a far more careful selection than is ordinarily made for children's reading begins with these first rhymes, which are to be given to the very littlest tots and cannot for that very reason be too carefully culled.

The selections in My BOOK HOUSE have been chosen for their music, their melody, their rhythm, their joyous nonsense, and quaint humor, their vivid flash of quickly moving pictures. The vulgarities, crudities, and twisted ethics have all been swept uncompromisingly into a dark closet and left there.

So, from the pages of My BOOK HOUSE, behold Old Mother Goose putting her very best foot forward, inviting you all with a curtsy, whatever the birth records may say about your age, to get your pipes and come skipping in her train, out where the meadows are always green, where lambs and children are always young, and the sun is ever shining.

THE ORIGIN OF THE FOLK TALES

From the very dawn of human history, men and women have loved to gather together in hut or castle, around the blazing camp-fire of the savage, or the homey hearth of civilization, and tell stories. Thus have arisen among all nations and peoples collections of tales peculiar to each particular folk, breathing the very spirit of their individuality and handed down orally from parents to children through generation after generation. These are the folk tales, which, at their best, in their vigor and simplicity, their vividness and beauty of imagery, the unaffected depth of their pathos and the irresistible drollery of their humor, form the largest and best part of children's reading, the characteristics that found their expression in the childhood of the human race, maintaining an eternal appeal to childhood all down through the ages. Our best known stories, Cinderella, Jack and the Beanstalk, Sleeping Beauty and many others are folk tales.

Although there had long ago been scattered collections of these tales, such as the wonderful Arabian Nights, from the Arabian and Persian and other oriental sources, first brought to the notice of Europe in the eighteenth century, and the collection of Charles Perrault made from the French in 1697, it was during the nineteenth century that men began to be especially interested in collecting these stories, taking them down carefully from the mouths of natives, and from them studying the customs and habits of thought, even the history of the various peoples. Most notable among these collections are those made by the Grimm Brothers in Germany, and Asbjörnsen and Moe from the Norse. We have collections of folk tales, however, not only from the German and Norse, the French and English, but likewise from the Gaelic, Welsh, Spanish, Scotch, Finnish, Italian, even from the Zulus and other African tribes, American Indians and Australian Bushmen. In fact we have collections from nearly every nation under the sun and most of the savage tribes besides.

From a careful study of these collections certain very interesting facts appear. In the first place, in every Aryan country, that is every country inhabited by the white race, even those separated by the widest stretches of land and sea, the incidents, plots and characters of the tales are the very same, a few incidents common to all being put together in an endless variety of different combinations. How has it possibly come about that peoples so far apart, so long separated by space, so widely different in language and customs, as the Germans and the Hindoos for example, possess the same household tales? Everywhere among the Aryans we find legends of the ill-treated but ultimately successful younger daughter, of which Cinderella is a type. Almost every nation has some version of the Cinderella story. Cinderella herself is French, coming to us from the collection of Perrault. The real English version is the story of Catskin. In German Cinderella is Aschen-puttel; in Italian she is Cenerentola. Likewise she appears in Norwegian, Russian, Hungarian, Servian, Irish and among the tales of any number of other folk beside.

As wide spread as the story of the victorious younger daughter, is the story of the victorious younger son. He is always despised by his elder brothers, and yet succeeds at various difficult tasks where the elders fail. Such stories are Boots and His Brothers, from the Norse, The Flying Ship, from the Russian, The Golden Bird, from the German, Through the Mouse Hole, from the Czech.

Again, everywhere are stories of the wife or daughter of some powerful and evil creature, a giant, a sea-serpent, a beast, a monster, who runs away with the hero to escape from the monster. The monster pursues and the fugitives delay him by throwing something behind them, a comb that turns into a forest, the branch of a tree that becomes a river and so on. Everywhere, too, are stories of men that have been turned into beasts by a charm and are rescued by the faithfulness and devotion of some maiden. Such are Beauty and the Beast from the French, East O' the Sun and West O' the Moon from the Norse, Snow-white and Rose-Red from the German, etc. Beasts, birds and fishes are capable of speech, as the Fox in the Golden Bird, the flounder in The Fisherman and His Wife. Even rocks and trees and other inanimate objects are capable of speech, as in Boots and His Brothers, and in all is the element of magic, resistance always giving way to the spell of certain rhymes or incantations.

It is scarcely possible to suppose that the similarity of these stories among so many different peoples can be explained by conscious borrowing, that the Scotch Highlanders for example read Russian tales or traveled into Russia and so copied Russian stories, since the common people, the peasants, who are the guardians of the ancient store of legends in every land, read little and travel less. More likely it is that long, long ago in the dim beginnings of history, when the Aryan race still lived as a single people, they already possessed many of these stories, and when they scattered from their original seat to people lands as far distant from each other as Ceylon and Iceland, they bore with them the germ at least of many of their household tales. Very possible it is too, according to Mr. Andrew Lang, that far back in the unrecorded wanderings of man, these stories may have drifted from race to race. In his introduction to *Grimm's Household*

Tales, Mr. Lang says, "In the shadowy distance of primitive commerce, amber and jade and slaves were carried half across the world by the old trade routes. It is said that oriental jade is found in Swiss lake-dwellings, that an African trade cowry (shell-money) has been discovered deep in a Cornish barrow. Folk tales might well be scattered abroad in the same manner by merchantmen gossiping over their Khan-fires, by Sidonian mariners chatting in the sounding loggia of an Homeric house, by the slave dragged from his home and passed from owner to owner across Africa or Europe, by the wife who according to primitive law had to be chosen from an alien clan."

Much of the similarity in household tales may be due to both these explanations, the common origin of the Aryan race and the unrecorded driftings of commerce, yet neither one entirely explains the matter, since many non-Aryan races possess the same tales and there is much similarity to the European tales in tales of races that have been utterly shut off from communication with the rest of the world, the Peruvians and the Aztecs in Mexico for example. Even the Cinderella story is not peculiar to the Aryan race. The first known version of it is the Egyptian story of Rhodopis and the Little Gilded Sandals.

The tale of the weak creature who runs away from a powerful and malevolent being, casting impediments behind to delay the pursuit of the monster, so common in European tales, is also particularly wide-spread in many non-Aryan countries. Among

the Eskimos a girl marries a whale. To visit her, her two brothers build a boat of magical speed. In their company the girl flees from the whale. The whale discovers her flight and gives chase but is detained by various objects which she throws at him, until at last she and her brothers escape and the whale is transformed into a piece of whalebone. In a Samoyed tale, two girls are fleeing from a cannibal step-mother. They throw first a comb behind them, as the mother is almost upon them, and that becomes a forest; other small objects become rivers and mountains. The same kind of feats are performed during flight in a story from Madagascar, and one from the Zulus. A Hottentot story tells of a woman's flight from an elephant. In Japan, the hero, followed by the Loathly Lady of Hades, throws down his comb and it turns into bamboo sprouts which check her approach.

The most probable explanation of the similarity in various folk tales that could not possibly be explained by transmission or a common origin, seems to be that this is due to the similarity of primitive man's imagination and intellect everywhere, no matter how separated by material barriers. Savages the world over, past and present, although utterly cut off from all association with each other, have invariably shared certain views of life. For one thing they draw no hard and fast line between themselves and the animal or inanimate world about them. To the simple mind of the savage, all things appear to live, to be capable of conscious movement and even of speech. The sun, the moon, the stars, the very ground on which he walks, the clouds, storms and lightning are all to him living, conscious beings. Animals have miraculous power and are supposed to be able to protect him as illustrated by the totems of the Alaskan Indians. Moreover, the savage believes infallibly in magic. Everywhere we find Australians, Maoris, Eskimos, old Irish, Fuegians, Brazilians, Samoyeds, Iroquois and the rest showing faith in certain jugglers or wizards of their tribes. They believe that these men can turn themselves or their neighbors into animal shapes, that they can move inanimate objects by incantations and perform all the other rigamarole of magic.

It is most likely therefore that the remarkable similarities in the various folk tales are chiefly due to the identity of early fancy everywhere. They originated undoubtedly while the races

were still uncivilized, and the unprogressive in each race preserved the old tale, while it is probable that those who forged ahead intellectually and acquired culture began to polish and perfect these old tales until they grew gradually into the myths that became the religions of the peoples.

Some of these old folk-tales, as has been contended, doubtless were told to explain natural phenomena, why the sun rose and set, how the thunder-storm came, what produced the lightning, but they were not by any manner of means all designed to do this, as some students of folk-lore have insisted, explaining Little Red Riding Hood and nearly every other nursery tale as a sun myth. Those that were an attempt at such explanation usually frankly declare themselves to be so. For instance the myth of the man who caught the sun and anchored it to the earth is a savage attempt to explain why the sun pursues a regular course through the sky, instead of going hither and yon at will, and is found not only in the Hawaiian, but among American Indians and New Zealanders as well.

The folk tales were rather as a whole a natural expression of primitive man's imagination and intellect, his views of life, his aims and interests, without particular purpose or meaning. Gradually as his life became better ordered and richer in experience, his intellect keener and clearer, his spirit more refined, certain simple moral conceptions began to creep into his tales. Thus men the world over in lands far, far apart began to express a natural love of good temper and courtesy by tales of the good boy or girl who succeeded in enterprises where the bad boy or girl, as a punishment for churlishness or disobedience, had failed. Such stories are The Twelve Months, from the Bohemian, Toads and Diamonds, from the French. Admiration for steadfastness and devotion began to express itself in stories of the maiden who keeps on through great hardships to free her lover from evil enchantment, as in East o' the Sun and West o' the Moon and the Russian counterpart of the same.

More and more, simple moral and ethical ideals, shared by all mankind, with no necessity for intercommunion to impart the same, the natural expression of man's growth everywhere, his higher longings and inner urgings began to form their own stories with a certain similarity among all peoples, and no one thing gives a better conception of the universal oneness of human nature, the similarity of its line of unfoldment everywhere than a glance over its old folk tales.

From the foregoing explanation of the origin of folk tales it becomes apparent why, with so many gems of beauty as various collections possess, there still exist side by side with these, hideous barbarities, crudities and cruelties, survivals from the savage days of the story's origin, step-mothers designing to eat their children, tempting them into chests and letting the lid down to crush in their heads, women cooking their step-children's hearts to eat them, mothers and fathers deserting their own children to die in the woods; and it also makes clear why no scientific edition of folk tales, that is, a collection made for purely scientific study, is fit for children. For their use the most careful selection and editing of the old stories is necessary that the truly fine and beautiful may be preserved and the false and gross eliminated. As the folk tales were told by all manner of people throughout generations, the story had always to be put in the words of the one who told it. Thus while he stuck closely to the outline and spirit of the story as it existed everywhere, he might vary it slightly to suit his own conception of what was finest and most beautiful in it, or omit that which to him was valueless or disfiguring. It is thus that all good versions of the folk tales have been told and it is thus that they are given in *My BOOK HOUSE.*

WHAT IS A MYTH?

A MYTH is a popular story intended to explain some natural phenomenon or some phase or problem of life. In general, a myth deals with the actions of gods, or beings possessed of divine attributes. It seems most probable that the myths were the outgrowth of the household tales and that, while the tales were preserved by the rude and uncultured among the races, the more advanced and intellectual of each folk refined these tales into the myths which gradually became the religions of the peoples.

While many of the myths are merely poetical and impossible, though beautiful, explanations of natural phenomena, as How the Sunflower Came, Why Winter and Spring Come Every Year, etc., mythology as a whole means far more than that in the evolution of human thought. As men in the very beginnings of ordered thinking, began to seek for causes beneath the outward appearance of things, to question and ponder instead of blindly accepting the universe, they could not escape striving to understand the power that creates, sustains and regulates the world, from which emanates the thought and life that pervades and animates all the universe; and, being unable to conceive of that power, so diversified in the infinite variety of its manifestations and operations, as one power, one God, they conceived of it as many gods; they perceived its various attributes and qualities as these appeared in human experience, and personified each of these as a god or goddess. Thus, when they perceived wisdom, truth, beauty, etc., to be vital and powerful elements of human life that must have a source somewhere, instead of conceiving of one God who is all wisdom, beauty, truth, bountifulness, productivity, strength, life, light and love, they conceived of a god or goddess who gave wisdom, a god or goddess who gave life, a god or goddess of beauty, a god or goddess of truth, bounty, productivity, strength, etc. Instead of one God whose power embraces the universe, there was a god of the earth, a god of the sea, etc., and humanity's innate perception of its own necessity for seeking divine help, help outside its own inadequate capacities, in time of trouble, expressed itself in seeking protection from the various gods, each of which was endowed with that protective power which belongs truly to God.

Thus early man's system of gods was only human thought in a state of evolution crudely and imperfectly recognizing the various attributes of the one God, naming and classifying the various unseen elements that go to make up life, commencing definitely, if slowly, to distinguish between good and evil. And back of their manifold gods, the myth-makers nearly all dimly perceived the idea of one power in an Odin or Jove who was All-father and supreme. It is said that the early Egyptian priests, though their religion always possessed far more points of dissimilarity than of similarity to the Hebrew, still possessed very distinctly this secret of one God, one Cause and Creator of the universe, and Mr. Prescott tells us in his *Conquest of Mexico*, that even the Aztecs, evolving their religion so utterly apart from the rest of the world, recognized, in spite of their barbarous myths of many gods, the existence of a supreme creator and Lord of the Universe. "They addressed him in their prayers as 'the God by whom we live,' 'omnipresent, that knoweth all thoughts, and giveth all gifts,' 'without whom man is as nothing,' 'invisible, incorporeal, one God, of perfect perfection and purity,' 'under whose wings we find repose and sure defence.' These sublime attributes infer no inadequate conception of the true God." He tells us furthermore, in *The Conquest of Peru*, "It is a remarkable fact, that many, if not most, of the rude tribes inhabiting the vast American continent, however disfigured their creeds may have been in other respects by a childish superstition, had attained to the sublime conception of one Great Spirit, the Creator of the Universe, who, immaterial in his own nature, was not to be dishonored by an attempt at visible representation, and who, pervading all space, was not to be circumscribed within the walls of a temple."

However much men still confused good and evil, sensual and spiritual qualities, in defining the nature of their gods, early mythology represents at least a pressing forward of primitive human thought toward explanations of the universe, toward some comprehensive grasp of the unseen force behind creation, and some attempt to sort out good from evil; and however great the jumble of superstitions with which the truth was still overlaid, each nation pressed just so far along this line of discovery as its particular thought was capable of reaching, untouched by the supreme truth which came with Christianity.

Early myth-makers personified not only the qualities and elements which they perceived to be good in human existence, but also those elements which they perceived to be evil, sometimes as gods, as in the case of the Norse Loki, god of mischief and evil, father of sorrow and death, but more often as hideous monsters, giants or trolls. In the Norse, these personifications of evil were often creatures of mist and darkness, of lies and illusion, which must disappear before the light, certainly, not an unintelligent conception of evil, and the Norse not only set forth in their myths the material warfare of warmth and light against cold and darkness, but they set forth also the warfare of good against evil. In the Persian, the Children of Light war against the spells and illusions of the Children of Darkness, the Deevs, and again, the material sense of light wiping out darkness, has the deeper meaning of spiritual truth and enlightenment wiping out evil.

In many of their myths the Norsemen reached a very lofty and beautiful conception of things. In the god Baldur, they honored all that was beautiful, eloquent, wise and good. He was the spirit of activity, joy and light. Even Thor, though he was degraded into a war god, seems at his best, in his encounters with the giants from the land of mists and winter, the land of lies and illusions, rather to have stood for that strong spiritual force that gives battle to evil, than a creator of strife among men, and his thunderbolt for no destructive force, but for that beneficent power that smites the chains of winter and sets free the life-giving showers of spring. The Norse attain a high spiritual level, too, in their conception of the final disappearance of this world, with the twilight of the gods, and the appearance of a new heaven and a new earth, an earth wherein goodness only dwells, an earth filled with abundance, regenerated and purified, where Baldur will come again with light and life, with wisdom, joy and goodness, and all evil ceases, for Loki is no more.

Though all nations have had their myths, and many, the East Indians for example, have an enormous jumble, the Greek and Norse mythologies are the most complete and orderly. The Greek myths show a love of beauty and brightness, of warmth and color, that makes the Norse look somewhat dark and somber by contrast, yet the Greeks retained far more of the sensuous element and attained far less of the spiritual than the Norse, and in selecting stories from the Greek to tell to children, this fact needs always to be borne in mind when selections are made. There are, nevertheless, many very beautiful Greek myths. There are the story of Hercules, his patience and his labors to free mankind from the various monsters, the myth of Echo and Narcissus, wherein the youth who loves only himself finds nothing but misery, unsatisfied longing and final death, the beautiful story of that dear old couple, Baucis and Philemon. All these and many others show true and right conceptions of things, and indicate that mythology, though it always remained a confused mixture of barbarism and beauty, with far more superstition than truth, and though it could never possibly have attained anything like the moral and spiritual height which a wholly consecrated, inspired, and persistent demand for truth did attain on the hills of Judea, holds nevertheless, when viewed in the right light, much beauty and much truth, which may be intelligently used for children.

THE WORLD'S GREAT EPICS

An epic is an heroic narrative, sometimes in prose, but most often in poetry, treating in heroic style a theme of heroic proportions. Its unity generally consists in the fact that all the incidents are grouped about one central hero. As the folk tales reflect the commonplace, homely, every-day life of the various nations and peoples, so their highest, loftiest, noblest, most stirring and deeply moving thoughts have been expressed in their long epic poems. These were told and sung by wandering bards in hall and castle from generation to generation, until at last some poet appeared, of sufficient genius to write down the tale and give it permanent form in the peculiar style and rhythm of his own country. In these massive old epics, with their splendid seriousness and dignity, their enormous breadth of canvas, their rousing stir of activity, and the frequent rise of their lines into passages of great and lofty beauty, we find the finest literature of each country, and in retelling stories from the epics, somewhat, at least, of this heroic style should always be preserved. Too frequently turning the mere story of the epics into prose has robbed the tale of all that enormous and splendid spirit that gave it its real life and beauty.

*GREEK EPICS

THE ILIAD AND ODYSSEY

THE greatest of all the world's epics—The Iliad and Odyssey—are attributed to Homer, who is said to have lived between 1050 and 850 B. C. Ever since the second century B. C., however, the question whether Homer was the originator of these poems,

**The Adventures of Odysseus by Padraic Colum. The Iliad for Boys and Girls by A. J. Church. The Odyssey for Boys and Girls by A. J. Church.*

or whether he merely recited verses already in existence, has been hotly disputed and it is probable that the Iliad was inspired by, or at least based upon previous poems. For centuries the Iliad and the Odyssey were publicly recited at gatherings of the Greek people, beneath the classic shadows of the Acropolis at Athens, in the stately marble porticoes of Greek dwellings, on the dappled lawns of temple groves overlooking the blue Aegean, and their splendid flowing lines, with their dignity and simplicity, have come down through the ages as the finest embodiment of Greek thought and spirit in existence, well worthy the race whose chief gift to humanity was the revelation of the gospel of beauty. The *Iliad* or *Achilliad* relates the happenings of some fifty days in the ninth year of the Trojan War, and the story all center about the hero, Achilles. The *Odyssey* is the story of Ulysses, or Odysseus as he is called in the Greek, after the fall of Troy and tells the story of his long ten years of wandering and his final arrival home.

*LATIN EPICS

THE AENEID

The greatest Latin epic is the *Aeneid*, written by Virgil in the first century A. D. It sings the wanderings of Aeneas, the Trojan, the heroic ancestor of the Romans, after he has escaped from the burning ruins of Troy. Since Roman literature was founded entirely on the Greek, the Aeneid is very closely akin in style and spirit to the Iliad and Odyssey.

†PERSIAN EPICS

THE SHAH-NAMEH

Next in antiquity to the Greek epics is the Persian, the *Shah-Nameh*, or Book of Kings, which was composed by the poet Abul Kasin Mansur about 920 B. C. Abul Kasin sang so sweetly that his master, the Shah, termed him Firdusi, or Singer of Paradise,

**The Aeneid for Boys and Girls by A. J. Church.*
†The Story of Rustem by Renninger.

by which name he is best known to the world. Mahmoud, Shah of Persia, who lived about 920 B. C., decided to have the chronicles of his land put into rhyme, and engaged Firdusi for this piece of work, promising him a thousand gold pieces for every thousand couplets he finished. Now, Firdusi had long wished to build a stone embankment for the river whose overflow devastated his native town, so he begged the King to withhold payment for the poem until the work was done, believing that the reward would then be so great that he could build the dike. But when the poem was completed at the end of thirty-three years, the Grand Vizier counted its 60,000 couplets and decided that 60,000 pieces of gold was too enormous an amount of money to part with, so he sent instead 60,000 small pieces of silver. On receiving so inadequate a reward for his long years of labor, Firdusi became justly indignant, distributed the money contemptuously among its bearers, wrote a poem stating in plain and none too complimentary terms what he thought of the Shah, and then fled from the land. It was not until after Firdusi's death that the Shah discovered the trickery of his minister and sent the 60,000 pieces of gold. As the poet's daughter refused to accept this tardy atonement, another relative took the money and built the dike which Firdusi had so longed to see.

Although the poem of Firdusi claims to be a complete history of Persia, it contains so many marvels, so many battles of the Kings with Deevs or devils (the Persian personification of evil) and is so involved and confused in incident, that were it not for its wonderful beauty of style and diction, it would scarcely have survived. The best stories in the *Shah-Nameh* are those dealing with Rustem, son of the white-haired Zal, and these are full of Persian flavor—of gardens and roses and nightingales.

*EAST INDIAN EPICS

MAHA-BHARATA AND RAMAYANA

Following the Persian we have the two great East Indian

**The Indian Story Book* (*Tales from the Ramayana and Maha-Bharata*) *by Richard Wilson.*

sacred epics, the *Maha-bharata*, and the *Ramayana*. The *Ramayana* was composed in Sanscrit some five hundred years before Christ, and is a strange mixture of the wildest and most preposterous legends with the truest and deepest philosophy. It relates events which are said to have occurred between two thousand and nine hundred B. C. The poem is generally attributed to Valmiki, a hermit who dwelt on the bank of the Ganges. One day it chanced that Valmiki saw one bird of a happy pair slain, and he made use of so strange and expressive a meter in singing the pity stirred in his heart at the sight, that the god Brahma, the one supreme God of the Hindus, immediately bade him employ the same meter in narrating the adventures of Rama. Now Rama is supposed to be one of the seven appearances in the flesh of the god Vishnu, the personification of the preserving principle among the Hindus, who, to protect the right, and punish vice and wickedness, in various epochs of danger appeared on earth in bodily form. Vishnu it is who at length will destroy all evil and restore mankind to virtue and purity. The foes of Rama in the *Ramayana* are the evil spirits by which Hindu mythology symbolized evil.

Like the *Shah-Nameh*, this poem is very long and involved as a whole, but out of it come many passages of the loftiest beauty —descriptions of nature that breathe the very heart of the tropical jungle, passages of the finest feeling, as for example, the one where Sita refuses to leave her husband in his exile. Its conception of the character of young Rama, too,—his love for his brothers, his devotion to his father, his modesty and humility, his control of his passions, his unfailing courtesy to his brothers' mothers, his devotion to his people, his tenderness for his wife, his steadfastness to his word, is one of remarkable beauty. Reading of this poem and frequent re-reading of it is regarded as a sacred duty by the Hindu. The *Ramayana* is his Bible.

THE LATCH KEY

*FINNISH EPICS

THE KALEVALA

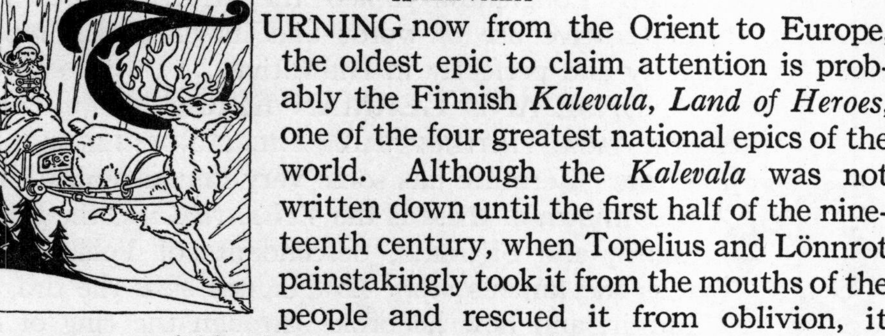

TURNING now from the Orient to Europe, the oldest epic to claim attention is probably the Finnish *Kalevala, Land of Heroes*, one of the four greatest national epics of the world. Although the *Kalevala* was not written down until the first half of the nineteenth century, when Topelius and Lönnrot painstakingly took it from the mouths of the people and rescued it from oblivion, it incorporates within it poems that doubtless date back some three thousand years into Finnish antiquity. The *Kalevala* relates the every varying contests between the Finns and Laplanders, Light and Darkness, Good and Evil, the Finns signifying Light and Good, the Laplanders Darkness and Evil. The story itself is both intricate and confused with a great multiplicity of events and characters. The chief and remarkable beauty of the poem is in its wonderful rhythm, its splendid flights of imagination and its occasional passages of high spiritual beauty, where, through the mist and confusion of primitive man's mythology, has penetrated a really inspired glimpse of the One Father, such, for example, as the prayers to Ukko.

The poet who sang the song somewhere in the dim past says,

> "*Nature was my only teacher,*
> *Woods and waters my instructors,*"

and certainly, the rhythm of the poem does ring and trip and ripple with the very spirit of winds and waves and woodlands, and any retelling of this fine old epic which fails to give some conception of the unique beauty of the rhythm, and its finest, most imaginative and beautiful passages, by no means does it justice, since the mere story of the *Kalevala* has nothing of remarkable beauty to commend it. It is the way it is told and the

**The Sampo, Hero Tales from the Finnish Kalevala, by James Baldwin.*

thoughts that have been engrafted into it which make it so wonderfully beautiful. Longfellow copied the strange rhythm of *Kalevala,* its alliterative use of words and its delightful repetitions, very exactly and perfectly in Hiawatha.

*NORSE AND GERMAN EPICS

VOLSUNGA SAGA, FRITHJOF SAGA, NIBELUNGENLIED

Norse literature has some very famous epics. The best known of these is the *Volsunga Saga,* the tale of Sigurd and Sigmund, descendants of Volsung. It tells the famous story how Sigurd slew the dragon, Fafnir, and how he broke through the ring of fire to rescue Brynhild, the Valkyr, from her long doom of sleep. The *Volsunga Saga* is also the source of the most famous German epic, the *Nibelungenlied,* the story of the accursed golden hoard of the Nibelungs or dwarfs, that brought such woe to Siegfried (the German Sigurd) and all who claimed it. But a more beautiful, though less known, Norse epic is the *Saga of Frithjof,* a story dearly beloved in Norway.

†ENGLISH EPICS

BEOWULF, THE ARTHURIAN CYCLE, ROBIN HOOD

IN English our attention is first claimed by the Old English *Beowulf,* which was doubtless composed before the Angles and Saxons left Europe and settled in Britain. Among the Angles and Saxons the art of poetry was very generally cultivated, and the harp was passed around to all at feasts that every guest might play and sing. Besides this, there were professional poets called in Old English, "scops or gleomen," who either travelled from place to place, or held permanent positions at the courts of chieftains or kings. These poets set out to sing of real events, but gradually they magnified the deeds of which they sang, and as the true event on which

**Siegfried, the Hero of the North* by Ragozin. *The Story of Siegfried* by James Baldwin. *Sigurd the Volsung* by Morris. *Frithjof, The Viking of Norway* by Ragozin.

†See foot note Page 195.

the poem was founded, receded into the past, the hero came to be pictured as enormously greater and stronger than he actually was, his deeds as infinitely more wonderful, until he became a sort of demi-god. Beowulf is held to have been a real person thus magnified, and stories about him arose among the Angles and Saxons in Europe in the seventh century A. D. These poems were originally heathen, and to this fact is due the mingling of heathen and Christian elements in the epic as we have it, for it was brought by the Angles and Saxons to England, gradually transformed as they became Christian, and written down at last by some Northumberland monk.

Though the scene of the poem is not England,—Beowulf was a Geat and his home somewhere in the Scandinavian peninsula, while Hrothgar was King of the Danes—it is decidedly and thorougly English in the social conditions it depicts, the ideals it presents, and the style in which it is written. It has great dignity and true elevation of thought, and the virtues which it exalts—courage, generosity, magnanimity, unselfishness, justice and courtesy, have always been particularly beloved in England.

Like all Old English poetry, *Beowulf* is not in meter. The characteristic of Old English verse was a line divided in the middle by a pause and marked by alliteration, two words in the first half of the line beginning with the same letter as one word at least in the second half of the line, as for example: "How deeds of daring were done by their athelings," or, "It burned in his spirit to bid men build him a dwelling." Another interesting and marked characteristic of Old English verse is the use of a phrase to imply a thing instead of the direct name for the thing, which makes for a most lively descriptive style and lends an interesting variety to the whole. Thus, the sea is the whale-path, or swan-road, the sword is the battle-friend, the harp is the pleasure-wood, armour is war-gear, a ship is a sea-goer, etc. In retelling the *Beowulf*, story-tellers should aim to give some idea of this

The Boy's King Arthur by Sidney Lanier. The Merry Adventures of Robin Hood by Howard Pyle. Northland Heroes (Beowulf and Frithjof) by Florence Holbrook. Una and the Red Cross Knight by Royde Smith.

most interesting and very distinctive Old English style. The entire poem consists of two distinct stories,—the first how Beowulf delivered Heorot from Grendel and his mother, and the second, how Beowulf, years later, delivered his own land from a dragon.

When Henry VIII, at Cromwell's suggestion, suppressed the monasteries in England, all the rich store of their libraries was scattered, much wantonly destroyed and lost. Some of the finest pieces of Old English literature were sold as old paper, used to scour candlesticks, to rub boots, or to wrap up grocers' bundles. It is a matter for which we may be very grateful, that in this general destruction, a single tenth century manuscript of Beowulf was preserved. This was injured by fire in 1731, so that the edges of the parchment are frayed and charred and many words and letters have disappeared, but the Beowulf still remains as the finest monument of Old English poetry, and a most interesting revelation of Old English thought and customs.

Next to be noted in the story of the English epic is the Arthurian Cycle, a number of epics or romances about King Arthur, the Knights of the Round Table and the ladies of his court. Arthur probably was a really good and noble Celtic King of Britain in the early days of the Saxon invasion, but his original character was gradually transformed by story-tellers until by the end of the twelfth century he had become merely an ideal king by means of whom chivalry could express its highest aims and ideals. There were likewise German, French, Welsh and many other versions of the Arthurian tales,—the German version by Wolfram von Eschenbach, the French by Chrétien de Troyes. The best known English version was by Thomas Mallory and all of these were written in prose. Tennyson's *Idylls of the King* are the Arthurian legends still further idealized and put into poetry.

Milton's *Paradise Lost,* Chaucer's *Tales,* and Spenser's *Faerie Queene,* are, of course, epics also, but they are the compositions of the poets who wrote them, not folk-epics like the others.

The beloved Robin Hood story was compiled from some two score old English ballads of various dates, some going as far back as the year 1400, and all full of the folk-spirit. In presenting this tale to children, it has always depended on how the story was told, whether it was sound or unsound, good or bad. If Robin Hood is presented as a thief and a robber, whom the child is invited to admire for his trickery and the ready use of his wit in questionable adventures, it is bad, but if he is presented as a true man of the sturdy and merry old English type, a lover of liberty and justice, who needs must be an outlaw in a period when the yeoman had no rights at all, and Justice abode not in the courts and laws of the land, it may be full of fine inspiration and feeling, as well as the joy of the free and glorious life in the greenwood. Though the ballads themselves contain many questionable adventures which it is necessary to recognize and avoid, no one can sympathetically read those old poems without loving their spirit, and feeling that the innate love of the English people for honest honesty, not conventional honesty, for justice and freedom, as well as the Englishman's unquenchable love for merry humor, were the inspiration of the original ballads, and suggest the key in which to pitch any retelling of the same.

*IRISH EPICS

THE CUCHULAIN

In Ireland there were three great cycles of poetry sung by the old Gaelic bards long years ago when Ireland was still pagan and had her own Irish gods. These cycles consisted of scattered poems never put into one great whole, and the finest and most Irish of them all is the one dealing with Cuculain or Cuchulain and the Knights of the Red Branch. Cuculain and his friends are historical characters, seen as it were, through mists of love and wonder, magnified into their gigantic stature just as all art

**The Cuchulain by Standish O'Grady. The Boy's Cuchulain by Eleanor Hull.*

magnifies, just as sculpture can create the gigantic statue of a man. The large manner of this antique Gaelic literature simply wipes out all littleness in its presence. Nothing small in the heart of man can stand before real sympathy with the enormous simplicity of this heroic tale of primitive Irish life.

Standish O'Grady was the first Irishman to reveal in a noble manner the greatness in this long neglected bardic literature of Ireland. He himself had the soul of an ancient epic poet, and as he carves out for us in sentences now charged with heroic energy, now beautifully quiet and tender, and always magnificently simple, the enormous figures of the Red Branch, we feel through and through that Cuchulain is indeed the true incarnation of Gaelic chivalry, its fire and gentleness, its hardy purity of mind, its largeness, its modesty and simplicity. Through the pages of O'Grady the ruddy chivalry of Ireland passes huge and fleet and bright, enormous images that loom as great as any among the epic heroes of the world.

*FRENCH EPICS

CHANSON DE ROLAND

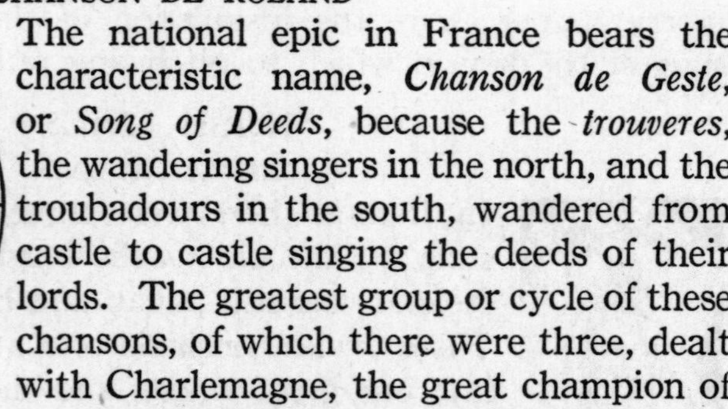

The national epic in France bears the characteristic name, *Chanson de Geste,* or *Song of Deeds,* because the *trouveres,* the wandering singers in the north, and the troubadours in the south, wandered from castle to castle singing the deeds of their lords. The greatest group or cycle of these chansons, of which there were three, dealt with Charlemagne, the great champion of Christianity, and his twelve faithful paladins or peers. When it was composed is uncertain, but the oldest copy now extant dates back to the twelfth century. The song, nevertheless, is much older than this. Like so many of the epics it was based on historical fact, later magnified and altered. The entire poem is

**The Story of Roland by James Baldwin. Frithjof and Roland by Ragozin.*

overhung and overshadowed by the dark and gloomy cloud of Ganelon's treachery, and no piece of literature in the world has more truly the feeling of the fearful ugliness of treachery than the *Chanson de Roland*.

*SPANISH EPICS

THE CID

In Spain the great epic poem as well as the oldest monument of Spanish literature is the *Poema del Cid*, written about 1200 A. D., a compilation from ballads already in existence, relating the story of Rodrigo Diaz de Bivar, called Campeador or Champion and Cid or Chief. The Cid was born between 1030 and 1040 A. D. and his heroic deeds were performed at a time when Christian kings were making special efforts to eject the Moors who had invaded Spain three hundred years before. Although the character of the Cid is, to our minds, defaced on many occasions by ugly deeds far from ideal according to our standards today, still the Cid's faults are largely results of the mistaken standards of his time and race, and in his virtues of kindliness, generosity, tenderness, courage, fidelity, he looms head and shoulders above the characters that surrounded him. Rarely has a man become the peculiar hero of a nation without some real virtues to commend him, and in the story of the Cid, nothing is more peculiarly his virtue than his devotion to his wife and daughters, which furnishes an incident well worth re-telling.

CHINESE AND JAPANESE EPICS

WHITE ASTER

The Chinese story of White Aster is scarcely an epic, but rather an idyll or romantic tale. Nevertheless, it passes both in Japan and China for an epic. It was written in Chinese verse by Professor Inouye and has been rendered also in classical Japanese.

**The Story of the Cid by Wilson.*

HOW TO JUDGE STORIES FOR CHILDREN

An Address

Olive Beaupré Miller

WHENEVER I am asked to make an address on the subject of children's reading, I always feel I want to begin by explaining that I speak not from the standpoint of a professor, a librarian, or a literary critic, but simply as one mother to other mothers, with such knowledge of the subject as I have gained from a most loving and sympathetic study of the nature of childhood at all the various stages of its development and a most earnest desire to bring to children all the good that is obtainable, holding every other consideration of small account beside the serving of the real interests of the child himself.

Although there has already been a great awakening to the importance of what the child reads outside the school-room, I feel that such reading is still regarded by too many parents as merely an amusement, of no great importance, with no object save to entertain the child. It is therefore held to be deserving of even less attention or supervision than his play. My earnest wish today is to get down beneath this superficial view of the subject, and place the whole matter of reading before you in its true light, as the very basis of your child's thought, of his views of life, of the moral and ethical standards he is forming, the spirit that is awakening and quickening in him, the character that is unfolding.

THE INFLUENCE OF IMAGINATIVE LITERATURE

What I have to say applies particularly to imaginative literature or fiction. I know the world has always taken more or less seriously the subject of scientific reading—reading of books on history, biography, science, etc. It has recognized the value of adding to the child's store of facts. I do not need to convince you on that point and so I am not referring to such books at all. Let the child read all of them he will; they are good for him. But it has been in the field of fiction that mothers and fathers have thought, "Oh, it doesn't matter much what Robert reads—it's only a story anyway!"

My friends, there are stories and stories and nothing matters much more than which story Robert reads. Robert may know all the scientific facts in the universe, may know the *Encyclopedia Britannica* backwards and forwards, and still never have perceived that selfishness, dishonesty, cunning, cruelty, weakness, narrowness of vision, are evil qualities which he does not wish to possess, and that courage and faith, strength and perseverance, honesty, loyalty, breadth of vision, are qualities which are splendid and admirable, which he does wish to possess.

In the settling of those great problems which have been stirred to the surface in the restless world of today and are facing the rising generation, problems needing greater wisdom and breadth of view for their solution than have ever faced the world before, is it going to be of more importance to Robert to know that the Battle of Hastings was fought in the year 1066 or to have innately and unconsciously acquired a love of justice and truth, an admiration for the big and unselfish view-point?

I am not belittling scientific reading; it is absolutely necessary and many a finely written history or biography may and often does accomplish the same thing as fiction, but I am bringing out as clearly as possible, that the value of the best fiction has been much under-rated and that because it has been under-rated, the best and most intelligent use has not been made of it in the child's development. The best fiction certainly will mould your child's ideals and standards, his views of life, his judgments on life, as surely as it widens his mental horizon, shows him other points of view than his own, quickens his imagination and his joyous appreciation of beauty, livens his sense of humor, deepens his emotions, and at every turn fires his spirit into life.

THE MESSAGE IN ALL GREAT FICTION

Thomas Hardy in his great novel, *Two on a Tower*, which doubtless many of you recall, gives a striking picture of the little, narrow, scientific mind, unillumined by that broad human sympathy which the best fiction awakens. The hero is the young astronomer, Swithin St. Cleeve, whose mental gaze is completely limited to the pursuit of further discoveries concerning the stars. He is absolutely unable to enter with any sympathetic understanding into the life and thoughts of those about him, and the havoc he works in the life of the splendid woman who loves him by always taking her literally, never being able to see what is not directly under his nose, to imagine or dream that she might be thinking or feeling something that she does not speak out, and that is not apparent on the surface, is a striking illustration of the point in question. If Lady Constance, from the height of self-abnegation, bids Swithin leave her because she believes his own good demands it, he obediently goes, without ever being able to realize that it is her own utter but unspoken sacrifice of self, not her pretended personal desires which bids him go, and that his going can mean nothing but sorrow and misery for her.

Always and ever it is only what is literal and apparent, to be discovered by the observation of the eye as one might discover facts concerning the stars, that Swithin St. Cleeve can understand, and one is deeply impressed by the perception that such a type of thought, though it might contribute a very learned article to the *Encyclopedia Britannica*, would be bound to spell tragedy in its human relationships, and indeed could never contribute to the world the most truly broad and useful service. And one wishes, wishes, wishes, that Swithin St. Cleeve had been steeped in fairy tales in his youth. What the world so sorely needs is thought, not only persistently seeking facts, but also infused and enlivened and enlightened by a broad human sympathy and understanding, a heart and soul capable of quick response to all those finer emotions that open the hearts of men outward, away from self to the needs of the world. And so we need both the encyclopedia and the story.

THE VALUE OF FICTION IN CHILDREN'S READING

JUST as the best fiction for us grownups—I am not speaking of course, of the mountain of trash that calls itself fiction in these days, but of such books as *Two on a Tower* and many another of its kind— just as that fiction gives us a truer knowledge of human nature, a clearer understanding of human motives, a broader, juster, more accurate and compassionate judgment of men and events, so does fiction do the same thing for the smallest child.

Beginning with his earliest fairy tales, the child commences to see in his stories, quite without any drawing of morals or particular direction of his attention to the fact, what qualities are splendid and noble, what qualities are base and ignoble, and for the very reason that the tale does entertain him, does interest him so intensely and move him to the very depths of his being, the impression left by the story is far more lasting and permanent than any sermon that could be preached on the subject, and constitutes itself an influence upon him greater than any other one thing which comes into his life, except the ideas and ideals that surround him in his own home, which, it must never be forgotten, leave the most telling marks upon his character. Hence the immense importance of always soliciting his admiration and sympathy for those qualities which are truly fine and never confusing his standards by holding up for his approval, trickery, dishonesty, cunning, deceit, and the rest of the train of evil.

It has been said that fairy tales give many children their first clear perception of the distinction between right and wrong, good and evil, and at their best this is certainly true. No child can sympathize deeply with the patience and gentleness and sweetness of Cinderella and hate the selfishness and vanity of the stepsisters, without all unconsciously registering a definite and lasting impression which forms a permanent part of his ideals.

Please understand, I am not arguing at all for the moral or moralizing tale—far, far from it, nor for definitely using stories to point morals, and so often destroying their art and the very qualities by which they charm the fancy and grip the heart. I am only saying that, by their very substance and content and spirit, the best stories do all unconsciously accomplish these results. The preachy, moralizing tale usually defeats its own purpose.

THE EVIL OF THE PREACHY STORY

ONCE, as a child, I got from an old-fashioned Sunday School library a book called *Willie Trying to Be Good*—I don't know what there was in the title that allured me, but anyway I chose it. Willie was a most self-righteous, unnatural, goody-goody little prig, and I had read no more than two chapters concerning Willie, when I wanted to creep up behind him and pinch him just to see if I could startle him out of his owlish primness by means of a perfectly natural "Ouch!" What was most remarkable about Willie was that he kept a great book and whenever anyone did anything kind for him he straightway ran and wrote down all about it in his book. Here he had neatly and accurately tabulated Mother, Father, Aunt Betsy and all the rest of the family, and then if Aunt Betsy did something which tempted him to be angry, instead of wickedly expressing his anger, he nobly restrained himself, went and looked in his great book under the index "B," found the name of Aunt Betsy and read all the good things Aunt Betsy had done for him, whereupon his anger departed and he betook himself to Aunt Betsy to deliver unto her a long and sanctimonious oration relating how he had been tempted and had overcome the temptation!

As I remember, on finishing the book I threw it across the room in such forceful disgust as to make a great deal of repairing necessary before it went back to the library, and the next time I was out of doors and thoughts of the saintly Willie popped into my mind, I picked a quarrel with a wholly innocent and inoffensive little neighbor girl, although I was by nature a peaceable child, just to show how different I was from Willie!

So I am not referring at all to books with a moral. I merely mean that all truly great literature worthy the name has expressed quite unself-conciously men's natural love and admiration for what is truly great and good and their natural perception of the ugliness of what is evil and false, and that this point of view, so inestimably valuable, is all unconsciously absorbed by the child, the very spirit of the work communicates itself to his spirit, *if the selections made for his reading are wise.*

THE DANGER OF UNSOUND LITERATURE

THOUGH *Willie Trying To Be Good* errs on the moralizing side, there are other stories sanctioned by the literary world because they have great literary beauty, which err as much on the opposite side, books which, in spite of their literary quality, are morally unsound and should be tabooed. Such a story is "Puss in Boots." The youth in "Puss in Boots," as you know, is a lazy good-for-nothing who wants a fortune in the world without working for it; and his cat, who is the hero of the tale, by a succession of lies, clever, cunning lies, gains for his lazy, good-for-nothing master an enormously splendid castle, a princess for his wife and succession to the Kingdom. The master is thus left revelling in material riches which he has done nothing to earn, and which have been acquired by clever dishonesty; and the child is left with the unconscious impression that the great aim in life is to be rich, and it doesn't make any difference how you attain that purpose, how clever and cunning and sly you may have been, so long as you get away with it and attain your object.

Does the world need any further encouragement to hang on to

such a distorted view? It certainly does not. And such stories, though of very great age and literary standing, should be allowed by intelligent mothers to die a natural death out of childhood literature. It is not that the influence of such a book is direct; it is not that if your child reads it he may go out tomorrow and commit some dishonest act; the influence is far more subtle and indirect. It is this—as he reads a succession of such stories, gradually the sharp, clear-cut edge is rubbed off his ideals and he begins to think that honesty is not such an important matter as he had imagined after all. Certainly the great evil of the world today is not that men are going about murdering each other wholesale. They are doing nothing so delightfully open in their dabblings with evil. They are merely refusing to face squarely the absolutely necessary separation which must be made between those qualities which are actually, absolutely, finally good, and those qualities which are actually, absolutely, finally evil, and so they are continuing in their smug self-satisfaction, their mental and spiritual laziness, to express in their various relationships and lines of activity, all the subtle dishonesty, selfishness, littleness, bigotry, superstition, conventionality, narrowness, envy, hatred and greed of a flourishing and unchallenged but well veiled and covered evil, that all too frequently wears the cloak of righteousness and respectability. In other words, the great need of the world today is for higher, more accurate and clearly defined ideals, and a far more consecrated determination to make a beginning at least, of putting these ideals into operation in all the varied activities of human life, from the least to the greatest. And I cannot too forcefully insist on the fact that we are utterly blind and unthinking if we continue to grind into our children's thoughts the twisted ethics of all too many among the stories that are offered him.

Matthew Arnold once splendidly defined true culture as the study of perfection, and he further defined perfection as an "inward condition of the mind and spirit" that results from "subduing the obvious faults of our animality" and bringing to light "the true ideal of beauty, of sweetness and light, and a human nature complete on all its sides." This, then, is the real aim of all true, honest, genuine culture, the bringing to light of a higher ideal of perfection, of a human nature complete, well rounded and balanced on all its sides. This means that intellectual culture must be everlastingly linked to moral and spiritual culture, that outward beauty of form must always be coupled with inward beauty of spirit. To attain such a culture should be the real object of all reading.

So let the heroes and heroines of the tales which you choose for your child solicit his deep sympathy and interest for the nobler qualities, for patience and perseverance, loyalty and truth, courage and compassion, and he will live those qualities with his heroes.

THE CHOICE OF FAIRY TALES

FAIRY tales, welling up from the simple, natural, untrained hearts of the common people, have been called the wild-garden of literature and they could not be more beautifully described. They are "the wild-rose in the hedgerows, the lily of the valley, the wind-flower, the meadowsweet, in contrast to the cultivated rose or gorgeous poppy that grows in the ordered gardens, beside the classic fountains of Literature's stately palaces."

But let us remember that in wild gardens there are weeds as well as beautiful blossoms, and so for our children, we need to weed out the weird and sensational, the unwholesome, the savage and morbid, and leave the pure and beautiful fancies, the vigorous, flourishing strength, the splendid, unself-conscious simplicity. There are many, many bad fairy tales and no one phase of your child's reading needs more careful supervision than his fairy tales. The sad fact is, too, that few editors have given you wholly satisfactory books on this subject, their judgment having been too frequently led astray by the literary beauty of certain undesirable tales.

I should never give a young child a whole volume of Grimm, Dasent, Asbjörnsen, Jacobs or any other literary collection of folk tales. They contain many horrible stories. If the child is to have these books whole at any time, let it be when he is older, say in the fourth or fifth grades, can read them without fear and has some ability within himself to throw off the evil that is there. Remember, a very young child refuses nothing—he soaks up every idea and impression—it is only as we grow older and our standards of life begin to assume some definite shape within us, that we sort out impressions that come to us, take the good and reject the bad. Choose rather a book of fairy tales carefully edited by someone who has truly understood young children and their needs. Let your fairy tales be as fanciful as you like—the child needs his flights of fancy; nothing great in the world was ever accomplished without imagination, and let these be the old folk tales, but let them be also wholesome, sound and true. All too frequently modern fairy tales, while they may lack some of the more objectionable features of the old stories, are sentimental and wishy-washy, and lack also all the splendid and convincing sincerity, vitality and strength of the folk tales. These old tales, properly weeded, still remain the real solid foundation for a child's reading.

A PLEA FOR TRUTH IN REALISTIC FICTION

NOW let us turn from fairy tales to realistic fiction, stories of events that might really have happened in actual life. We have seen that the most imaginative and fanciful fairy tale may be true, not true to material fact, but true to right ideas and ideals, and now when we come to realistic stories let us demand further that these stories be actually true to human experience. Let us ask that their characters be not abnormally good or bad, that the happenings be not exaggerated, but that they deal with real live boys and girls. I do not mean boys and girls glorying in mischief and many of the tricks thought necessary to make a child's book interesting; I mean worth while children, but not impossible ones.

And here you have whole hosts of books to avoid. I am sure I do not need to caution you against the sensational, racy, hair-raising ones, but I do want to advise you against the sentimental, wishy-washy ones, which are so often called "safe" because the evil in them is less apparent. These books give children no adequate view of human experience and its problems as they are really going to find them, but substitute weakness for strength, and delude them into the belief that life's victories may be cheaply and easily won, thus giving them no preparation whatever for the real, steady, persistent effort that success in any line will demand of every man. Such books are trash—only littering up children's mental store-houses.

Books in series are almost always of this type. In my childhood Horatio Alger was the chief representative of the series type—Sink or Swim, Live or Die, Survive or Perish. There was always a rich boy who was hideously villainous and a poor boy with a halo of righteousness about his head, and the poor boy always suffered the most dreadful outrages at the hands of the rich boy, but in the end the poor boy always grew marvelously rich and the villainous rich boy became marvelously poor, which gave the saintly poor boy an opportunity to be most superhumanly magnaminous, forgive the rich boy and restore him to his own again. When you've read one of those books you've read them all. They make no demand whatsoever upon your intelligence. Reading them gets to be a habit—one becomes a regular serial drunkard and imbibes at least one a day. Don't encourage your child to get that habit.

INSIST UPON REAL LITERATURE

NOW just one word more. Be sure that a book is well written. You may think this matter is not particularly important beyond its effect on your child's use of the English language, but it is. Often the subtlest, most indirect influences are the greatest. The very order of a well-written book influences a child, its unity and beauty, while a sloppily written story tends to induce disordered sloppy thinking. It is the literary perfection of a story which pricks a child's soul to new hunger and thirst after beauty and perfection.

Occasionally, a book of fine contents, poorly written, is worth-while, and I admit I would far rather my child would read a badly written book the substance of which was good, than a literary classic the substance of which was evil, yet our aim should always be well-written books. Help your child to select such books, do all you can to urge him to read them and to avoid the cheap and trashy stories. Talk to your boy or girl about the books he reads. Get interested in them yourself, keep his confidence on that point and you will find you are actually discussing with him the most vital problems of life.

FOR A HEALTHY MENTAL DIGESTION

Remember, whenever you see your boy or girl with a book, that the quality of that book is at least as important as the food you serve him. Would you give him impure food? No! Would you give him sloppily prepared food? No! Would you clutter up his digestion with all sorts of useless pastries and cakes and candies? No! Would you give him wholesome, nourishing, well-cooked, well-balanced food? Yes! Then do the same for his mind. The books he reads are his mental food. He swallows the ideas that form the substance of those books as surely as he swallows meat and potato. If his digestion is good he eliminates the evil and absorbs into his mental system the good. Those ideas which he absorbs circulate through his mind no less certainly than blood through his body, and he gives them out again as mental energy in the form of the motives that prompt his every act. How important it is then that the ideas fed him should be pure and his mental digestion be kept healthy. What is a sound body without a sound mind to govern it? The late war gave an example of the havoc that can be wrought by sound physical bodies without right ideals and standards to move them. We want no more of that for the welfare of the world. The future is going to make great demands on our children. Let us do all in our power to have them prepared to meet those demands and let us by no means neglect the proper use of so powerful an agency for good in their development as the world of books.

MY BOOK HOUSE

After closing this general discussion on the subject of children's reading, in which I have aimed to give you some few principles for judgment and selection, I have been asked to say a few words about My BOOK HOUSE, the carefully selected collection of stories and poems for children on which I have spent the past four years, and which I undertook through discovering for my own child what a chaos the field of children's literature was, what a mixture of good and bad, of gems and trash, and how great and universal was the need for such a work. In these books I have endeavored to collect the best stories and poems for children from the literature of all ages and all peoples and to embody in them the principles of selections which I have just been describing to you.

THE THREE TESTS

FIRST I have always asked myself, "Has this story literary merit?" If it has not, there is no need of going further. If it has, I have then asked secondly, "Will it interest the child?" If it will not interest him, what difference does it make how great its literary merit may be? If it has literary merit and will interest him, my third question has been, "Will what it adds to his life be for his good? Is its underlying idea true, does it present sound standards, is its spirit fine, its atmosphere healthful?" Many a good story has failed to pass this last test, but so far as my judgment and understanding goes, I have always applied it rigidly.

A story having then passed all three of these tests I have next asked myself, "What is the best age at which to present this tale to the child, the age at which he will get the most out of it?" And so I have tried to grade the stories as intelligently as possible.

PROPERLY GRADED STORIES

Remember we can never be too old to appreciate a piece of good literature. Many a dear old grandmother writes us apologetically that she enjoys the first book, *In the Nursery* as much as her smallest grandchildren, and I always feel like writing back, "Oh you dear grandmother, of course you enjoy Mother Goose and all those delicious, simple, joyous, nonsensical old tales, for the spirit of childhood is eternal in the human heart. 'Except ye become as little children ye shall not enter into the Kingdom of Heaven.' One or one hundred, what is the difference—the Kingdom of Heaven certainly consists in having the heart of a child!" One can never be too old for good literature, but one may be too young.

The proper grading of stories from this standpoint is one of the most important questions to be considered in the discussion of children's reading. A story that will make a most sound and healthful impression on a child of eight may be absolutely unhealthful at three or five. Very seldom has a good collection of stories been produced for children from the age of two to five—and this because few people, except mothers, really understand the little tot at this period, and most mothers of children at that age have something else to do besides write or edit stories. The child then is as different as possible from what he is when he begins to go to school or kindergarten. He is a little bundle of laughter, giggles and sunshine, and yet he is the most solemn creature on earth. His sense of humor is almost nil, or, rather, what is funny to him is not what is funny to grown-ups. He takes life tremendously seriously. He has as yet no philosophy with which to overcome any little sorrow, and he knows almost nothing of the great problem of evil with which he will one day be called to cope.

We have recently had a little nephew visiting us, a thoroughly sturdy, boyish little fellow about two and a half years old, not the kind one would ever accuse of being abnormally sensitive. As he sat on his mother's lap she often read to him:

"Three little kittens
They lost their mittens
And they began to cry;
'O mammy dear,
We sadly fear
That we have lost our mittens!'
'What! lost your mittens,
You careless kittens,
Then you shall have no pie,'
'Mee-aw, mee-aw, mee-aw!'
'No, you shall have no pie!'
'Mee-aw, mee-aw, mee-aw!' "

To watch that child's face as his mother read was a study. He followed the fate of those kittens with a breathless intensity and troubled concern worthy at least of Eliza crossing the ice with a pack of bloodhounds at her heels, and the relief, the radiant smiles that blossomed forth on his little face when those kittens found their mittens and got their pie were illuminating, all indicating quite clearly that much deeper tragedy than that which befell those three little kittens would be quite beyond his present powers of endurance. What a child will laugh at most heartily and see the humor of at six or seven is deadly earnest to him at three. And while we want quick response from children to all the nobler sentiments, to pity and compassion, as well as to joy and love, we will never overplay their emotions. To do this makes them morbid, sensitive and nervously excited. That is why at this period we need to be so particularly careful.

Now the understanding of such a state of thought, the sympathetic grasp of a very little child's viewpoint, seldom comes to anyone but a mother, and even with us mothers that understanding is the most evanescent thing in the world. As our own children grow older, acquire some sense of humor and some philosophy, we ourselves forget what these children thought and felt at two. But it has been my steady aim never to forget it or belittle it, to take it rather into intelligent consideration, and uncompromisingly demand that stories for the little one at this period be full of joy and sunshine and his own beautiful simplicity.

The child needs as yet to have very little to do with the problems of evil. That and its overcoming which lend strength to books for older children, can and must be presented to him gradually. Moreover, make it a general rule never at this age or any other to give a child a book which you think will leave him with a sense of fear, with a sense of evil as some great, mysterious awful power from which he cannot escape. Such a sense kills all endeavor. Stories should always lead him to feel that he can come out on top and have dominion over evil. It is this that spurs him on to resist evil.

WHEN THE CHILD IS YOUNG

CHILDREN ordinarily start school, that is kindergarten, when they are about five years old, and their thought begins then to be systematically guided and directed in right lines and channels, but what about those precious years before the child starts school? Should his thought at that time be left unguided and undirected? Should he be allowed "just to grow up"? Those first formative years are among the most important in the child's life and offer the most fertile field possible to the mother for moulding his thought by means of good stories and implanting in him, from the very beginning, sound and true views of life. During those years she is the sole guardian of his reading. Later, even as early as seven or eight, he will begin to select his own stories. What more important then, than that she should sow all the good seed possible while she is able to do so, thus forming the foundation of a sound character and of good judgment in his later selection of books?

Mothers begin to sing nursery rhymes and lullabies to their babies when they are a few days old. They should have at hand easily accessible for their use the very best. Why not let the child hear nothing else but the best? Does it make any difference that at first he does not understand the words? The very rhythm, music and melody of the good rhymes and lullabies soothe, quiet and train him. Why not let a child's ear for poetry be thus trained from the very beginning and so give him something good instead of something bad from the cradle?

IN THE NURSERY

THE first volume of My BOOK HOUSE, *In the Nursery*, has been very carefully worked out to meet just this need of the youngest child, and is perhaps as remarkable for what it excludes as for what it includes. It is made up of a most careful selection of nursery rhymes, leading on gradually to the very simplest rhythmic stories, demanding at each step a little more attention and concentration, a little more and a little more, till the child is led on naturally to listen to the more complicated stories. The child's next need after Mother Goose is always for these short rhythmic stories in prose, stories of the simplest possible plot, construction and wording. It is not yet possible to hold his attention on one subject for any great length of time, and the charm of rhythm is still a great factor in the appeal for his interest.

In The Nursery has almost no fairy tales. The child is as yet so young that the supernatural element confuses him. He is just learning the real world about him, and does not know where to place fairies and elves. I once met a little boy of three to whom a volume of Grimm was being read. He was a delicate, peevish, overwrought little creature and had fairies and angels and Santa Claus and God all in a hopeless muddle. So the stories and poems in *In the Nursery* deal with the actual world to which the child is just awakening, and are crammed full of the beauty and joy of earth and sky, of wind and sun, of bird and bee and flower.

ON THROUGH MY BOOK HOUSE

The second volume, *Up One Pair of Stairs*, is designed to expand the child's thought, give him stories of child life in other countries, and introduce to him the more simple fairy tales.

The third volume, *Through Fairy Halls*, is distinctively the book of fairy tales, gathered from the folk lore of almost every nation in the world. The child has now reached the age when fairy tales will no longer confuse him, when you can safely and most profitably give them to him. Quite unconsciously he now feels the fairy as a great spiritual force for good, always appearing at just the right time, to restore justice, to aid and protect virtue, to offer golden opportunities; and as unconsciously he feels the trolls and giants and monsters to be examples of evil, of cruelty, overbearance and bestiality, with whose wiping off the slate he heartily and rightly sympathizes. As these evil creatures are most useful in symobliz-ing to the child all those qualities which he does not want, we need only, in dealing with them, avoid the pitfall which makes many writers, in their anxiety to make ugliness appear ugly, make it so hideously ugly as to be terrifying. This is unfortunately true of many giant stories. The important questions always are, What is the impression this story is going to leave with the child? What qualities is it going to call out in him? If the story has left him with a sense of terror, and appealed only to his love of the sensational, it has accomplished nothing, and while we can by no means afford to compromise with bestiality and make it appear less than ugly, we still must be wise and sane in our dealing with this question.

Thus the third volume, *Through Fairy Halls*, is chiefly fairy tales, but it is well balanced, as are all these volumes, with good, realistic and humorous stories, since the child should at no time be allowed stories all of one type, lest his thought grow one-sided.

The Treasure Chest, is the book of adventure, progressing from the more adventurous fairy tales to realistic adventure.

From The Tower Window, is the book of romantic adventure. and its basic material consists of stories from the great national epics.

In this manner each one of the five volumes represents a distinct phase of the child's development. The last volume, *The Latch Key*, contains all the explanatory material which has been reserved for this book in order that no smallest note of adult or professional thought might mar the childlikeness of the other volumes.

ART AND ARTISTS IN MY BOOK HOUSE.

WHATEVER material we have used throughout the collection we have invariably aimed to present from the child's standpoint, so he would love the books. Accordingly, we have made much of the matter of illustrations and cover, by which the books first catch his attention and charm him through the eye. The influence of art for good has long been recognized, and the soul of the child filled full of the love for beauty has far less room to admit any ugliness than the soul of the child to whom hideousness seems natural.

The same careful consideration given to the editorial preparation of My BOOK HOUSE has been adhered to in its art. In the illustrations throughout there breathes a joyous childlikeness. The colors, while invariably interesting, are never flashy, gaudy or disquieting, but always harmonious and restful. The artists contributing number many of our best known illustrators. They were, nevertheless, not selected for their prominence, but because of the strength of their individual appeal to the child, and their particular suitability to the subject in hand. Thus, instead of letting any one artist do all the work, we have always selected *the* one particularly suited to the special subject of each story and, as a result, My BOOK HOUSE is a remarkable collection of the work of America's foremost illustrators for children, at their very best.

To sum up everything, we have tried, as intelligently and lovingly as possible, in My BOOK HOUSE, to give the child the best literature obtainable, to gather it from a very wide variety of sources, covering many ages and many peoples, that his thought might sweep out broadly, to grade all this material as intelligently as we could, and to put it forth in such form that it would be irresistible.

MY BOOK HOUSE

INDEX OF AUTHORS, TITLES

*First edition †Second edition

THE LATCH KEY

AND IMPORTANT CHARACTERS

M Y B O O K H O U S E

THE LATCH KEY

THE LATCH KEY

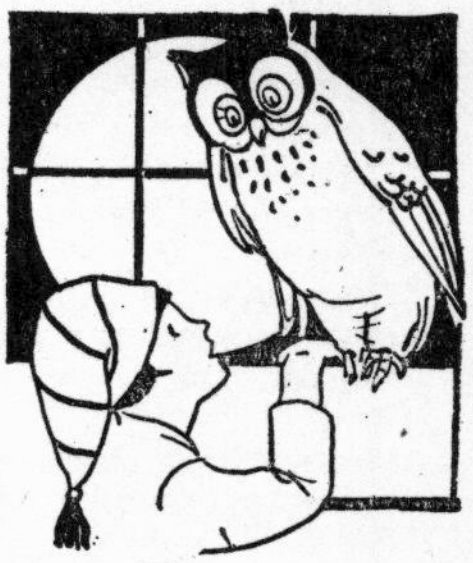

THE LATCH KEY

THE LATCH KEY

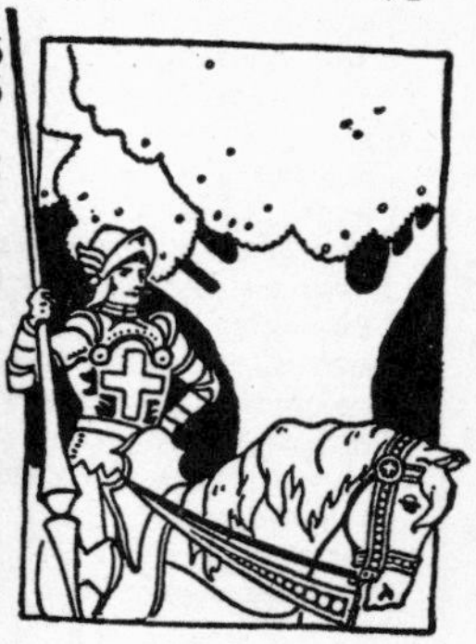

GEOGRAPHICAL INDEX

For the use of those Mothers, Fathers or Teachers whose children ask for a story about Spain, Italy, Japan, etc.

THE LATCH KEY

THE LATCH KEY

THE LATCH KEY

MY BOOK HOUSE

HISTORICAL INDEX

***Indicates First Edition †Indicates Second Edition**

It is remarkable, that involuntarily, we always read as superior beings. Universal history, the poets, the romancers, do not in their stateliest pictures...anywhere make us feel that we intrude, that this is for our betters; but rather it is true that in their grandest strokes there we feel most at home. All that Shakespeare says of a king, yonder slip of a boy that reads in a corner feels to be true of himself. We sympathize in the great moments of history, in the great discoveries, the great resistances, the great prosperities of men.—*Ralph Waldo Emerson.*

THE LATCH KEY

THE LATCH KEY

MY BOOKHOUSE

SPECIAL SUBJECTS INDEX

For the use of the mother, father or story-teller whose child asks for a story about a little dog, or a fox, or an engine, or for a funny story, or a fairy story, or a true story.

* First edition. † Second edition.

THE LATCH KEY

ANTELOPE

GIRAFFE

KANGAROO

REINDEER

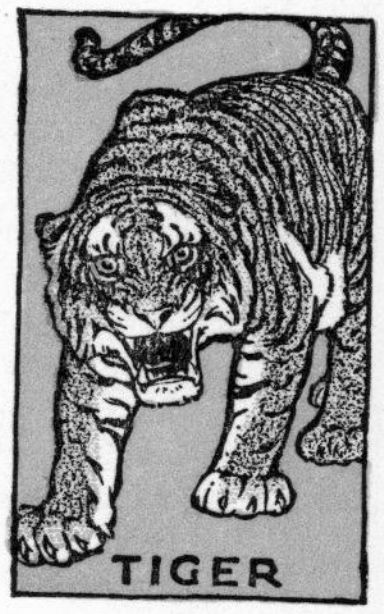
TIGER

COCKATOO

OSTRICH

VIKING SHIP
Used by the Norsemen in raiding England

ROMAN TRIREME
Vessel with three banks of oars

QUEEN ELIZABETH'S FLAGSHIP THE ARK ROYAL
Built in 1587 for Sir Walter Raleigh Purchased by Queen Elizabeth and used as her flagship in the fight with the Spanish Armada, 1588

STATE BARGE OF THE DOGE OF VENICE
Used in ceremony of Wedding the Adriatic

EARLY STEAM AND SAILING VESSEL
The first ocean steamship

THE LATCH KEY

THE LATCH KEY

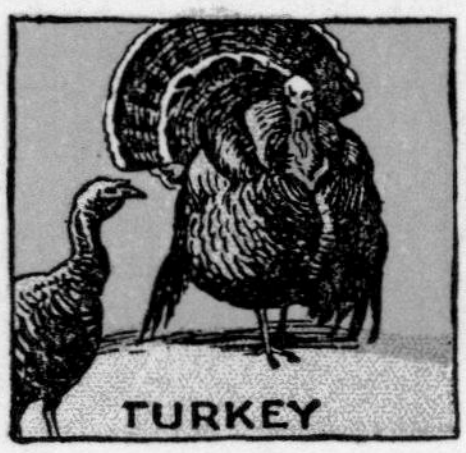
TURKEY

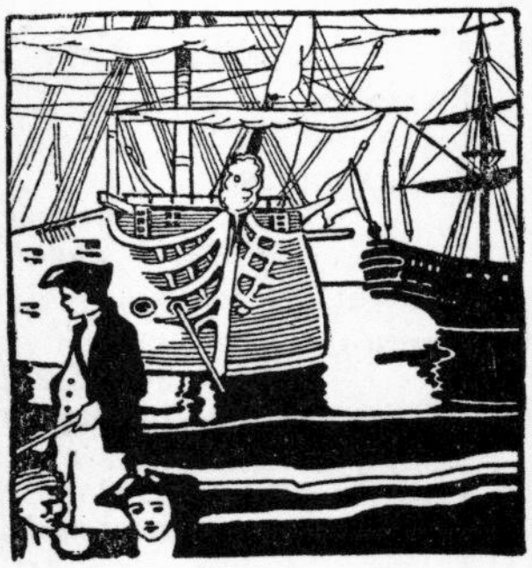

INTRODUCTION TO INDEX ACCORDING TO ETHICAL THEME

I am weary of seeing this subject of education always treated as if "education" only meant teaching children to write or to cipher or to repeat the catechism. Real education, the education which alone should be compulsory means nothing of the kind. It means teaching children to be clean, active, honest and useful.—John Ruskin.

Real education certainly is a spiritual as well as an intellectual process. It certainly does mean guiding children to see clearly the distinction between good and evil, right and wrong, moving them deeply with sympathy for the good and repugnance for the evil, and inspiring them to act in accordance with these perceptions. This is rarely accomplished by preaching at children or moralizing to them. But all good stories and books have recorded naturally and most often unconsciously the reaction of the author or story-teller to various human qualities and types of human disposition, and through his art, indeed by his very unconsciousness of what he is accomplishing, the story-teller makes the child feel deeply just what he has felt. If the author has felt affectation, artificiality, boastfulness, conceit, as ridiculous qualities, he makes them ridiculous; if he has felt cold self-righteousness, cowardice, dishonesty, hypocrisy, treachery as ugly qualities, he has made them ugly, and the child vigorously separates himself from them and refuses them as he reads; if he has felt courage, compassion, loyalty, truth, devotion, perseverance, purpose as splendid qualities, he has made them splendid and the child has felt them to be splendid and desired to possess them in every fibre of his being. It is not that such an author tells the child these qualities are thus and so, whereby he could do no more than make a pin prick of an impression on his intellect; he moves him to *feel* that they are so in the very depths of his spirit wherein he truly lives and moves and has his being, and so leaves a lasting impression upon him

> *A man is not educated because he buys a book; he is not educated because he reads a book, though it should be the very best book that ever was written, and should enumerate and unfold all the law of God. He only is educated who practices according to the laws of God.—Horace Mann.*

It is thus that truly worth-while books and stories mould children's ideals. But besides this general shaping of their standards there is an addition a specific use which the father, mother or teacher may occasionally make of the stories. If a child has been unkind and discourteous, to read him such a story as Toads and Diamonds without any comment whatsoever, is often the most effective remedy for the trouble. If he has been unloving, the beautiful story of the love of little Snow White and Rose Red for one another may do more for him than worlds of preaching.

And so, quite without spoiling the stories, or detracting at all from their right purpose to amuse and entertain, one may often make this particular use of them with remarkably good results. It is to meet this particular need in the most intelligent way and in answer to many requests that the following Index According to Ethical Theme has been prepared.

To live for common ends is to be common,
The highest faith makes still the highest man,
For we grow like the things that we believe,
And rise or sink as we aim high or low.—Robert Browning.

MY BOOKHOUSE

INDEX ACCORDING

* First Edition. † Second Edition

THE LATCH KEY

TO ETHICAL THEME

COURTESY

THE LATCHKEY

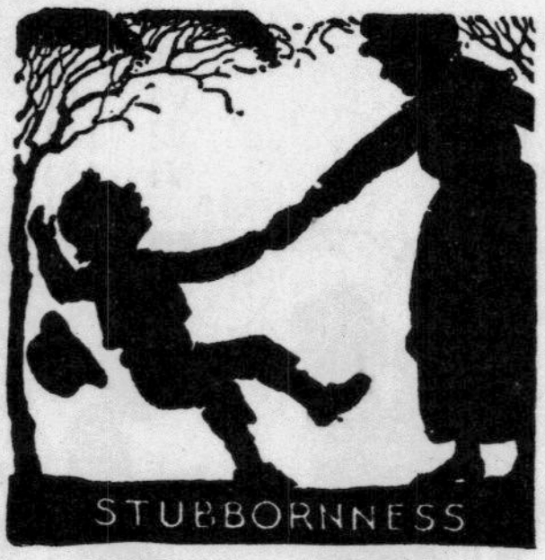
STUBBORNNESS

WORSHIP
TIMIDITY
TEMPER
WISDOM